I'M THE GIRL
WHO WAS RAPED

Published in Canada by Inanna Publications, Toronto, 2017
in conjunction with Spinifex Press, Victoria, Autralia, 2017
First published by Modjaji Books, Cape Town, South, Africa, 2016

We gratefully acknowledge the support of the Canada Council for the Arts and the Ontario Arts Council for our publishing program. We also acknowledge the financial support of the Government of Canada.

Printed and Bound in Canada.

Cover design: Val Fullard

Thank you to Susan Hawthorne for permission to include her poem "How do you protect yourself from rape?" first published on project365plus.blogspot.com.au ©
2016.

Library and Archives Canada Cataloguing in Publication

Hattingh, Michelle, 1988-, author
        I'm the girl who was raped / a memoir by Michelle Hattingh.

Previously published: Cape Town, South Africa: Modjaji Books, 2016.

Issued in print and electronic formats.
ISBN 978-1-77133-445-7 (softcover).-- ISBN 978-1-77133-446-4 (epub).--
ISBN 978-1-77133-447-1 (Kindle).-- ISBN 978-1-77133-448-8 (pdf)

        1. Hattingh, Michelle, 1988-. 2. Rape victims--South Africa--Biography.
3. Rape--South Africa. 4. Victims of crimes--South Africa--Biography. 5. Sex
crimes--South Africa.I. Title.

HV6569.S7H38 2017   362.883092   C2017-905381-7
                                                   C2017-905382-5

Inanna Publications and Education Inc.
210 Founders College, York University
4700 Keele Street, Toronto, Ontario M3J 1P3
Telephone: (416) 736-5356 Fax (416) 736-5765
Email: inanna.publications@inanna.ca Website: www.inanna.ca

I'M THE GIRL
WHO WAS RAPED

A MEMOIR

MICHELLE HATTINGH

INANNA
Memoir Series

FOREWORD

BETTY MCLELLAN

THE BOOK YOU ARE ABOUT TO READ describes every woman's nightmare and many women's actual experience. Rape. It's a sad fact that, even in this so-called enlightened twenty-first century, women's reality is that we could be raped at any time (from infancy to very old age) and in any circumstance. Here, South African woman Michelle Hattingh is heartbreakingly honest as she recounts her own experience of rape and its aftermath.

In every nation on earth, men's predatory sexual behaviour is so commonplace that rape is seen by many as 'normal' and 'to be expected'. It is for that reason that, when it happens, blame can so easily be placed on the victim. Why wasn't she more careful? Why did she make herself so vulnerable? That women are all too often heard expressing an inability to relax around men, that a woman must always be on guard in case a man (friend, husband, stranger) decides to violate her, is a sad indictment of the male of the human species.

For many decades, feminists have wondered out loud why so many men interpret the male privilege afforded to them by patriarchy as giving them entitlement to access women's bodies without consent, and why so few perpetrators see any need to consider the consequences their forced sexual intrusion will have on their victims.

Prompted by the findings of detailed research undertaken by feminists, women have spoken out with confidence against men's violent sexual behaviour. Naming it for what it is, Susan Griffin wrote in 1971 that:

...rape is a form of mass terrorism, for the victims of rape are chosen indiscriminately, but the propagandists for male supremacy broadcast that it is women who cause rape by being unchaste or in the wrong place at the wrong time – in essence, by behaving as if they were free. (35)

Susan Brownmiller wrote that rape "is nothing more or less than a conscious process of intimidation by which all men keep all women in a state of fear"(15). Michelle Anderson refers to rape as "sexually invasive dehumanization" (643), while Robert Jensen concurs with the feminist understanding that rape is the sexualisation of power and adds that "rape is about the fusion of sex and domination, about the eroticization of control"(80).

A serious disappointment for feminists who have worked diligently to "break the silence" on sex crimes has been that there appears to be no appreciable change in the attitude and behaviour of many men. It was hoped that, by bringing the previously hidden crime of rape out into the open, raising consciousness about the devastating effects on victims, and focusing on the need for equality between the sexes, men would come to understand that women's bodies were not theirs for the taking. Feminists believed, perhaps naively, that most men were capable of developing an understanding of the notion of women's autonomy and that a respect for women's rights would follow. Among the many examples proving that not to be the case is that of high profile former England footballer Adam Johnson who is currently serving a six-year sentence in a British prison for sex offences with a fifteen-year-old girl. At his trial, he apologised and claimed to feel ashamed but, after one year in prison, he was secretly filmed sharing his true thoughts and feelings with other prisoners.[1]

It wasn't his fault. He did nothing wrong, he said. Along with crude comments and gestures about his victim, he is heard regurgitating every myth imaginable about rape and sexual assault. Referring to his six-year sentence in response to a fellow prisoner's remark that he didn't actually rape the girl, Johnson says: "No, I wish I fucking did—for six years." He shows no remorse, only anger and self-pity. "The most startling thing about

Johnson's rant," said Joan Smith in a report for *The Guardian*, "is his belief that men are the real victims in rape cases, at risk of being falsely accused by women who are too drunk to remember a sexual encounter."

When a woman who has been raped has the courage to name it for what it is and report the offence to the police, the blaming of the victim begins. Myths are recited by the perpetrator, his supporters, his legal team, and others in the community who refuse to believe men are capable of such behaviour. It was just sex, they say. She asked for it. She obviously wanted it. She was too ugly/fat/old/etc. to be raped. She had been drinking and put herself in a vulnerable position. She encouraged him, led him on, and then changed her mind. The victim-blaming often extends to actual verbal abuse as Adam Johnson's young victim expressed in her Victim Impact statement:

> I had to face so much abuse.... I was made out to be a liar.... The gossip on social media and hearing all the horrible names that people have been calling me has been devastating to me, my friends and family. (Morley)

For rape victims generally, the victim-blaming and verbal abuse is just the beginning of all the negative effects they experience. There are invariably emotional effects that can include feelings of shame, humiliation, self-blame, PTSD, depression, anxiety, fear and suicidal thoughts. Also, there are physical and behavioural effects, for example, a dependence on alcohol and/or drugs, sleep disturbance, nightmares, venereal disease, and unwanted pregnancy.

Many of these effects were mentioned by victims/survivors of rape and sexual abuse in a national survey conducted in 1992 by the Australian Institute of Criminology. The survey was carried out with a view to discovering the prevalence of the crime in Australia and its effect on respondents. The 2,852 responses contained harrowing stories of incest, marital rape, rape by ex-partners, date rape, rape by acquaintances, bosses, doctors, priests, and others in positions of trust, as well as stranger-rape.

Patricia Easteal, Senior Criminologist at the Institute, brought the women's responses together in her acclaimed work *Voices of the Survivors*, which provided an opportunity to dispel the myths and put an end to the widespread practice of blaming the victim. While the myths and victim-blaming have not gone away, the survey enabled respondents to tell the story of their rape experience (some, for the first time) and to feel supported and affirmed by those who received their stories. One victim/survivor, expressing her relief and gratitude wrote: "Scared silent. Let us finally be heard" (Easteal 14).

The report contains many stories of young teenage girls coerced or threatened by boyfriends, betrayed, and, in some cases, handed over to "mates" who took turns raping their victim. There are stories, too, of women being raped as adults by colleagues in the defence force, by police, employers, priests and others who are assured of the woman's silence because they know she is fully aware of the fact that no one would believe her. Michelle Hattingh was raped by a stranger. Regardless of who the perpetrator is — boyfriend, colleague, acquaintance, husband, or stranger—the impact of rape is so profound that, for many women, it is the thing that defines them, at least for the foreseeable future.

Amy (not her real name) was fourteen years old when she was raped in Geelong, Australia, on 1 November 2015. Three men, brothers, were arrested and committed to stand trial on multiple rape and related charges on 9 June 2016, but the trial was discontinued in February 2017 when Amy and her family decided that Amy's mental health was more important than winning a court case. Amy's sister said: "My sister is traumatised by what happened and would have had to relive it again on the stand, knowing every word would be scrutinised and held against her" (Perkins).

At sixteen, Amy confided in the journalist that she couldn't wait to finish high school and begin her studies at university. She said, "I can't live a normal teenage life any more. Teenagers all have their labels: the sporty girl, the party girl. I'm the girl that got raped" (Perkins). It's interesting to note that Amy's words are almost exactly the same as the words Michelle chose for the title of this book. Compare Amy's: "I'm the girl that got raped" with Michelle's: "I'm the girl who was raped." It's an identity that a rape victim puts on herself because she is aware that the people around her who know about the rape also think of her in that way. And this "identity" that a rape victim carries with her creates confusion. She desperately wants to ignore it, to avoid re-living the terror and pain of what happened but, at the same time, she needs to talk about it because it has become who she is.

Amy did talk about it—to her parents, her sister, a member of the Victorian police force who is described as a "professional, empathetic female sergeant" (Perkins), sexual assault workers, lawyers, and her psychologist. The decision Amy made to discontinue the trial, to refuse to offer herself up to be brutalised all over again by the processes of the law, was a good decision, made in the interests of preserving her mental health.

Michelle spoke about her experience too and received the kind of love and support she desperately needed—from her mother, rape crisis workers, and friends. As a university student majoring in psychology, she knew that an important next step toward her recovery would be to participate in a sexual assault survivors' group where she could share her trauma with other women who had been through similar soul-destroying experiences. The mutual support would have aided her recovery but, sadly, there was no such group available to her at that time.

For all rape victims, recovery requires that they take a series of steps away from the unbearable isolation they feel. The first step is to tell at least one other person who they feel certain will be sympathetic and supportive (a relative, friend or counsellor). The next step is to tell more people, including the police if they want to prosecute. A third step is to join a sexual assault survivors' group if one is available. All of these steps will help rape victims work through their trauma to the point of then being able to tell the world. When fear and shame have been replaced by anger and determination to expose the prevalence and severity of rape, then healing has begun.

Writing this book must have been as difficult and traumatic for Michelle Hattingh as it was therapeutic. The task she set for herself was to re-live every sordid detail of the rape so that she could tell her story honestly and combine it with her analysis of the experience, not as an observer but as the victim struggling to survive and heal. Reading this book is not for the faint-hearted because the author very skilfully draws her readers into her experience. We are made aware of her thoughts and feelings as the rape is happening, her fear, her revulsion as well as her relief that she is still alive when it's all over. She takes us along with her, too, on the difficult and painful struggle toward healing.

To feminists everywhere who despair that men continue to downplay their rape crimes and blame women victims, this powerful book offers hope. *I'm the Girl Who Was Raped* presents a much-needed opportunity to raise the level of understanding in society of the concept of women's right to authority over their own bodies. Michelle Hattingh's frank account reminds us that, one day, when women behave as if they are free, it will be because we *are* free.

Betty McLellan is a feminist ethicist, author, psychotherapist and committed activist of long standing. Her current involvement with the North Queensland Domestic Violence Resource Service enables her to combine her work as a psychotherapist with a broader emphasis on feminist ethical analysis and activism. She lives in Townsville, Australia.

ENDNOTES

[1]The video was posted to the Internet, but has since been taken down.

WORKS CITED

Anderson, Michelle J. "All-American Rape." 2012. *St. John's Law Review*, 79.3 (2012): 643. Print.

Brownmiller, Susan. *Against Our Will: Men, Women and Rape.* Ballantine: New York, 1975. Print.

Easteal, Patricia. *Voices of the Survivors.* Spinifex Press: North Melbourne, 1994.

Griffin, Susan. "Rape: The All-American Crime." *Ramparts Magazine*, September 1971: 35. Print.

Jensen, Robert. *The End of Patriarchy: Radical Feminism for*

Men. Spinifex Press: North Melbourne, 2017. Print.

Morley, Nicole. "Adam Johnson says he wished he had raped underage girl in sick prison video." *Metro News*, 21 April 2017: np. Web.

Perkins, Miki. "'I'm the girl that got raped': How a family coped with a teenage daughter's ordeal." *The Age*, 21 March 2017: np. Web.

Smith, Joan. "The rape boasts of Adam Johnson show victim-blaming is still with us." *The Guardian*, 21 April 2017: np. Web.

HOW DO YOU
PROTECT YOURSELF FROM RAPE?

SUSAN HAWTHORNE

She asks him,
  How do you protect yourself from rape?
He is silent for a long time.
He says,
  I avoid going to prison.

She asks him again,
  Do you want to know what I have done or have avoided
  doing?
He is silent again.
Then a nod.

She says,
  I don't talk to strangers.
  I don't go out alone at night.
  Or if I do I have my keys at the ready.
  I have my running shoes on.
  I look as if I know where I'm going even when I don't.
  If I do go out at night, I listen.
  I listen for the footsteps behind me.
  I judge their heaviness, their gait.
  I consider whether the footstepper is female or male.
  I try not to run.
  I look casual.
  Or, I turn and look him in the eye.
  The advice is contradictory.
  I take self-defence classes.

I become a black belt.
And still I don't feel safe.
I lock the windows too.
I have a fisheye lens in the front door of my flat.
When I go out with friends, I don't drink too much.
I don't leave a half empty/half full glass to come back to.
I don't accept a lift home.
I catch a taxi instead.
I have a sensor light outside my house.
My dog is just the other side of the door.
I don't allow anyone to take my photograph.

Have I been successful?
No.
Once, I drank too much.
Once, I accepted a lift.
Once, I talked with someone I knew.
And among my friends
One was married to a rapist.
One found out the man beside her was raping her
daughters.
One was touched all over by the man next door when she
was five.
One was followed on the street.
One found pornography on her lover's computer.

I asked them what they did to protect themselves from rape.

One said:
      I don't talk to strangers.
      I don't go out alone at night.
      I set my mobile phone to speed dial.
      I have my running shoes on.
      I look as if I know where I'm going even when I don't.

One said:
      When I go out at night, I'm careful.
      I stick to places that are well lit.

If I hear footsteps behind me
I try not to run.
I look casual.
I take out my mobile phone
I ring my friend.

One said:
I take self-defence classes.
These days I teach self-defence to women.
And still I don't feel safe.

One said:
I have a dog, a big one with a deep bark.
I have three locks on my door.

One said:
I don't do social networking,
I don't want anyone knowing too much about me.

Were they successful?

No.
None of them.

For all rape survivors

1.

THE BREEZE SLIPS THROUGH THE CAR WINDOW and runs its fingers through my hair. The gin bottle jiggles in anticipation in the passenger seat next to me. I twist and turn the wheel through everlasting roads, trying unsuccessfully to hurry to the party. My headlights strike into the night. The Cape Town mountains are barely discernible in the darkness.

I slow down as I enter Muizenburg. Houses surround me and my sense of solitude drifts away. Amala, ever the mother, messages me to find out where I am. *Almost there!* I reply as I look for the house.

I see a cottage with a balcony spilling onto the pavement. Young people mill about with drinks in their hands, absorbed in each other. Hazy lights and the bouncy sounds of electro-pop music accompany them. They are dressed in the uniform of millennials just about to break into the world of responsible adult life: jeans, dirty hair, languid movements exuding a whiff of anticipation. I park next to the party and walk away from it. It's obviously too cool to be the one I'm supposed to attend. Away from the crowd, the street narrows and the sharpest sounds are barely heard before they get swallowed by the night. It is deserted. I square my shoulders and look for house number twenty. I walk further and further into the dark. I touch empty walls. The lights, the music, and the people are behind me. I am alone.

"Michelle!"

I turn around.

"Michelle!" A madman at the party not only knows my name but he is waving his arms in a very enthusiastic manner.

Oh! I recognize the madman as Kieran, a fellow Psychology Honours student. It turns out the party I walked away from is where I'm meant to be. It's our end of year party – where we celebrate the fact that we survived Psychology Honours. And where we acknowledge that we had given up our sanity in the process. Relieved, I run to the house. As I walk up the balcony steps, a small woman in a pink Power Rangers suit hurries to me.

"Julia!" I yell. She crushes me with a hug. Julia is the kind of person who uses the word "rad" un-ironically—even in defence of her staunch feminist hypotheses. When we met, we bonded over our passion for feminism and our shared talent for being awkward. Everyone knows us as the two girls who sit in the back corner and never stop talking during lectures.

"Why aren't you dressed up?" She glares at me. I was supposed to come as a Tinky-Winky from the Teletubbies.

"Friend, those costumes are insanely hard to find. But I did bring this—" I reach into my handbag for my pink diamond tiara and place it on my head. "Ta-da!"

I hug my other friends. There are twenty-seven of us in the class. We survived academic, mental and emotional torture and our elation is similar to that of soldiers who survived battle. We embrace in the way you do when you know your time together is ending. On the balcony, there is a spread of drinks and brownies. I grab one, the first piece of food I've had all day.

"Let's get you a drink!" Julia says as I stuff my face.

I nod. "Wow, Nikki's house is amazing!"

"I know, it's right on the beach," she says as we walk inside. It's open concept. The furniture inside the living room has been pushed to the side, and a little disco ball is hanging from the roof. It throws pinks, greens, and yellows onto Julia's nose. A foosball table separates the living room and the kitchen. People play on it enthusiastically. Their elbows stick out at right angles and they pause only to take a swig from their precariously balanced beers between goals. The kitchen table is littered with more food and bottles of alcohol. Empty peanut butter, marmite and jam jars act as glasses.

Life, and all of its disappointments, sits in the corner, watching and waiting for us. But not yet. Not tonight.

"Mich, I was getting worried!" Amala comes over and gives me a hug. She is wearing what she always does: a golf t-shirt, jeans and sneakers. Her thick black hair is shoved behind her ears.

"I'm so sorry! I fell asleep, then I overslept, and then obviously I got lost, and then I tried to walk away from the party I'm supposed to be at, but it's okay—I'm here!" I hug her.

Malini smirks at me. Malini and I became friends because of our mutual love of sarcasm. We were drawn to each other but neither of us knew why. I come across as a cheerful, frivolous person, and Malini tries very hard to come across as a bitch. We saw through the other's façade with the ease of a person who has years of experience in putting on masks.

"Let's drink!" I announce.

"Here we go," Julia hands me my drink, which she spills on me in her enthusiastic delivery.

I take a sip. Gin and tonic with a hint of peanut butter.

We dance in a big circle underneath the disco ball. The music distorts, and we jump on the couches. I practice my white-girl booty-pop—impressive since I don't have a booty to pop. I lose Julia and see her leaning against a wall with David, who is a trance party fiend from our class. She smiles widely at him, eyes partially closed. I wonder if that's her flirt face or her drunk face. Malini and I grind against each other while Amala takes photos of everyone and everything.

I walk outside to cool off and chat. The salty sea air stings my nostrils and electro beats are now the background to our conversation.

"I still can't believe what you did today," Nick, the coolest guy in our class, says to me. There are only four guys in our class, but still. Nick has the ability to make dumb words sound intelligent, which is why I like him.

I smile at the memory of what happened earlier.

"Wait, what happened? I keep hearing about it but I wasn't there. I just heard Shane saying that one of the students said all men are rapists," asks Allie, a woman with long curly blonde hair.

Everyone looks at me. I clench my teeth in irritation.

"Well, basically, at my presentation today, Shane was stirring up stuff about how I was saying any man can rape, when that was just the title of my thesis, and something one of my participants said, and not what I was saying at all, so…" I shrug.

"She demolished him," Nick says.

I don't want to talk about it so we move on. Allie, Nick, and I debate religion. At most parties, controversial topics like religion, politics, and rape probably won't come up. At a party with Psychology students you don't really find us talking about things that are not controversial. With regards to religion, they are atheists and I'm not.

"But how can you justify believing in God when there is so much evidence against Christianity?" Nick says. He clearly thinks I'm an idiot.

"Listen, I've read all of that stuff. I know that most of Christianity has pagan origins, and I'm not idiotic or close-minded enough to think everything I read in the Bible is true or perfect. But, in my life, I've had too many experiences with things that I can't explain. With powers that are too great to be simplified to a coincidence, and I consider myself extremely lucky to have experienced those things. I think everyone chooses to translate this power in a different language, some call it God, others call it Buddha or energy or science or choose to close their minds to it. I just can't."

I don't know if my words make sense or not, but it doesn't matter. A bit later, a group of us walk to the beach. It's about twenty metres away from the house. We stride into the brisk night air. We climb over rocks to get to the beach until we see the ocean. Nick and I sit on the rocks with a few other people.

We laugh and laugh and talk about nothing at all. Malini's shoes get wet, and she walks back to the house.

"Loser!" I shout at her back. "People in this day and age have really lost their adventurous spirit." I sigh in mock disappointment.

She gives me the finger.

The wind whips through my jacket, and the sea sprays softly on my cheek. I breathe and feel alive and happy. I have survived one of the hardest years of my life, and I kicked ass.

In the distance, Julia grabs and kisses David. Their passion overwhelms them to the extent that they meet the rocks head-first more than once. The rest of us, as appreciative spectators, cheer them on. The waves are a strange, luminous green colour. It is one of the most beautiful things I have ever seen.

Around midnight, I am tired, sober, and ready to leave. I have only slept for about three hours in the past two days. I am physically and emotionally exhausted. I am also sick of people. I just want to shut out the world for a couple of hundred hours.

As I think this, one of the girls comes up to me. It's one of the other students. This girl doesn't want me to use her name, or describe her, and so I won't. From now on she'll be "my friend." It could have been any one of them.

"Mich," she touches my arm. "Can I speak to you?"

She looks down as she says this. I grab her hand and lead her outside. We squish close to each other on a beanbag out of earshot from the rest of the party.

"So, what's up?"

"I have to tell you something."

"Okay."

"When I was listening to your thesis today, it just brought up some stuff. While I was listening to you speaking, I didn't want to be there. I felt so uncomfortable."

It's clear she has something on her mind. While conducting interviews for my thesis on rape, several girls came to me and asked to be interviewed. Even though my study focused solely on male students, these female students ignored the instructions and came to me anyway. It was always because they had experienced some type of sexual abuse. One girl had been raped three times by three different men from her local community. Their stories were different, but they all spoke with the same sense of urgency. They wanted—*needed*—to be heard.

As she starts to talk, another girl from our class comes and sits down with us.

An awkward silence follows.

"Do you want to go for a walk?" my friend asks me.

"Sure, of course."

We walk away from the party. We follow the path to the beach and sit on a bench on a grassy patch that leads to the sand and rocks. We can almost hear the music and laughter from the party.

As she starts telling her story, I look over her shoulder and see two well-dressed men heading in our direction. I don't think much of it when one of the guys comes and sits on the bench next to us. It irritates me, but it doesn't scare me.

"Are you tomboys," he asks, but it's not a question. His white teeth flash, a stark contrast to his dark skin. He leans his upper body over his knees, folding his hands together in a cavalier manner.

This is obviously some kind of lingo but I have no idea what he's talking about.

"Are you lesbians?" he asks.

Now I get it.

"No," I say defensively. The other guy is standing behind us and we can't see him. The guy who speaks to us is well-dressed in jeans and a leather jacket. The only rational thing to do in these situations is to get out. I am not scared. I am irritated with these guys for interrupting our important talk. I want to protect my friend.

"We are leaving now," I say, getting up assertively.

"No, no, we'll go," he says, and they start to walk away.

For a moment, I am relieved. This is always how these situations end. Always. They walk about twenty metres away, and I see them standing and talking about something. The waves continue to spray over us.

"Mich, I'm scared," my friend says.

"It's fine, don't worry, we'll leave now," I'm irritated with her for being scared. Haven't I been in similar situations hundreds of times before? All we need to do is get out of there. I turn around from looking at them. I can't see them. Then I hear them walking back to us, and I know.

I know.

They are on us. One grabs my friend, his knife against her throat. The other lunges next to me. Flashes his panga knife. Hands are on my bag. They are shouting. I won't let go of my bag. I fall to the ground. He tries to jerk my bag away from my body. My heart is in my head.

This isn't happening. This isn't happening.

"Give me!" He holds his panga over my body.

I let go. I have no idea what's going on with my friend. I can't see her.

This isn't happening. This isn't happening.

He opens my bag. He takes my cellphone, my wallet, my GPS. "Take their jewellery," the other one says. The one with my friend. He is in charge.

The one who is with me grabs my fingers. Flesh touches. Rough, shaking. Him or me? Jerks my ring off.

"Give, give!"

I shake as I take off my watch. My necklace. He puts on my ring. My watch. He is wearing my jewellery.

Look at his face. Remember his face. They will want to know what he looks like.

I stare and stare and stare. He rifles through my bag. From his hand, the panga dangles—lazily, carelessly. The panga drops. He catches my eye.

Do it.

The thought is in my head before I can stop it, irrational.

But this isn't happening. I'm not strong enough.

Do it.

I grab it. He looks at me, shocked. I am more shocked than he is. I lift the panga and thrust it into his arm. I scream. I hope my friend will follow my cue and fight back.

"Aaaaah!"

My hair is pulled out of my skull. The other one kicks me. He kicks me again.

"Stupid bitch!" He grabs the panga out of my hand. He swings his leg into my curled-up body.

"I will kill you!" He kicks me. Kicks me again.

My friend screeches. She hasn't moved.

"Don't hurt her!" she screams.

He yanks me up by my hair to a sitting position. The guy who I grabbed the panga from stares at me. Without blinking, he punches me in the eye.

I feel nothing. I am surprised. I thought getting beat up would hurt. This was little more than an itchy bite.

Give me more. I can take it.

"I will kill you, stupid bitch!" The other one stands over me. "I have killed for less! Listen here." He grabs my shirt and pushes his face against mine. "I killed a man, knifed that white fucker! For less than what you do! I kill you!" His breath smothers me.

He means it.

"Drag her over there," he tells the other one, pointing to a patch of sand next to the wall.

My guy pushes me there. I lie down on my back.

Michelle. It's really happening.

I start sobbing. I cry because I am scared. I cry because I want them to feel sorry for me.

"IF YOU CRY I WILL KILL YOU!" He spits into my face. His spit joins into the snot and blood already there. I stop without a sound. Without looking at him.

I don't know how else to manipulate them.

They pull my friend down next to me.

I know I am supposed to memorise what their faces look like, for later. So I try.

I can't concentrate.

Okay Michelle, they are going to rape you now.

Okay.

Don't be here. Leave. Michelle, they are going to rape you NOW. Leave. Okay.

The one who stole my bag comes to me. He undoes my pants. He yanks them down to my knees and pushes my legs apart. He yanks down my underwear. The sand rubs against my bum. He undoes his own pants. He lies down on top of me. His body anchors me to the ground. He isn't heavy. I do not fight. I know that if I do anything they will kill me.

I am not here.

"Are you a virgin?"

To tell the truth, I don't know if I am. I've had some uncertain experiences in my past. But I know I have to say yes. If I'm not a virgin, they could think that I have sexually transmitted diseases or AIDS. And I doubt that they're about to whip out some condoms for a safe rape experience. At this stage, I want him to rape me. Rather rape me than kill me. Use me. Don't kill me.

I hear my friend say "yes" to the man who lies on top of her.

"Yes," I say.

"Good, I am a virgin also. Put it in."

I'm confused.

"Put it in, ja."

I understand. I reach down. His penis is hard, slippery. Firm. I put it inside of me. I struggle to get it in.

"Put it in or I kill you!"

I have to spread my hips to get it in. He starts to move.

In, out.

I am not Michelle.

This isn't happening.

I look at the stars. They are bright, beautiful.

I am not a daughter.

In, out.

I am not a friend.

In, out.

I take my friend's hand and squeeze it. Hard. She squeezes back.

Is it happening?

Of course not.

In, out.

I am not a lover.

He lifts my arms and folds them into an awkward embrace around his neck.

I am not a person.

God? Are you there, God? Where are you?

In, out.

I am not a woman.

His tongue swirls around my cheek. Hard but soft. Wet. His breath comes in gasps. The night smells still, smells fresh.

In, out.

I am a female thing.

God? God! I need you!

And then they are done. I don't know if he came inside of me.

This isn't happening.

"Tie them up," the other one says.

The one who raped me gets two pairs of shoelaces out of his jacket pocket. Shoelaces that he carries around with him. He ties one pair around my wrists and the other around my ankles. Our two rapists chat while they tie us up.

"Ek het daai wit man dood gemaak. Ek het my mes gevat en nou's hy dood," the one who raped my friend says as he carves up her panties in order to tie her hands with them. I wonder if he is teaching the other one how to rape. He knows more and does everything first. Now he's explaining to him how he killed the white man: "I took my knife and now he's dead."

They pull and drag us to the rocks. I struggle to move because the idiot tied my feet together. My jeans are still around my knees.

"Come, hurry, come!" He shouts at me, "I will kill you if you slow!" I can't move because he tied me up but he will kill me if I don't move.

"Trek haar broek op!" The other one shouts. The one who raped me comes and attempts to pull up my pants.

We lie on the rocks. The waves crash all around us.

"Sorry ladies, sorry for this," they chorus.

"If you try to get up and run away, I will throw the rocks at your head until you are dead. If you lift your head, if I see you, I will throw rocks at your heads until you are dead. I don't want to kill you but I will," my friend's rapist announces. He's cheerful.

They leave.

We face each other. She is crying. I am looking at the stars. The rocks push against our tender bodies, sharp edges digging into our bruised forms.

Don't let me die.

Don't let me die.

Don't let me die.

"We have to get out of here," I tell her.

"Where are our friends? Why aren't they looking for us? Where are they?"

"They're not going to come."

We have to save ourselves.

"Let's undo these."

I push and tear at the shoelaces around my hands. They won't come off. My heart pounds. I struggle. They won't come off.

Eventually, I take her hands and undo her shoelaces.

I forgot that we can help each other.

"Now do mine," I tell her. She gets them off.

My body is shaking and everything inside of me tells me not to do this because when I do it they will see me and come back and they will kill me and I will die I will die and I don't want to die I don't know what to do but I don't want to die, but still I push myself up on my elbows and grind my face into the muddy hill in order to see whether they are still there.

Their parting words pump blood into my ears: "If you lift your head, if I see you, I will throw rocks at your heads until you are dead." I blink across the rocks. They are still there, smoking.

"Get down!" I fall back. "Tie them back on. Tie them on!"

I am scared they will come back and see that we tried to untie ourselves. That they will get mad at us. That they will kill us.

"We can't go. We have to wait." I say. There is no way we can outrun them. We are bruised. We are sore. We are in shock. If they see us trying to escape, they will come. They will kill us.

"Where are our friends?" my friend asks.

"They're not coming. We have to be strong."

We lie on the rocks and wait.

My mom won't be able to handle it if I die. I don't want to die. I'm not ready. I'm still supposed to do something with my life.

They'll think it was my fault.

We hold each other and wait for death. I think they are taking a smoke break. They are taking a smoke break, and then they will come kill us.

No one can ever know about this. We will escape, go back to the party and forget this happened.

The sky sparkles. I try to tell myself like I did with the rape: *you are now going to die. They are going to kill you.*

NO.

I can't do it. It doesn't work with death.

With the rape it worked. I knew that they were going to rape me; I could prepare myself for it. But death ... I'm not ready to die. No matter how insignificant my life ends up being from here on out.

Where are you? I shout to God.

We lie there for the whole of eternity. On those rocks we die. We shed everything that we are and we know. We fall off of our-selves like crumbs, and cleave to the rocks, to be lost in darkness forever. We are not born again. I realise I am dying. I do not accept it but it is not up to me. Someone else decided. You do not know what the complete absence of hope, faith, and love looks like until you see the look of someone else deciding whether or not you should die. Rape is not something. It is the absence of everything. And we shed our lives, our dignity, and I shed my love on those rocks.

Crumbs to dust. We lie, and the rocks consume us. "Michelle!"
In the distance.
"Michelle!"
Louder. Our friends are coming for us!
I pull all of me together. I use the last bit of myself to get up. And I scream. I scream and scream. I see Nick, Kieran, and Julia. I scream. Snot and tears mingle and flood into my open mouth, they melt onto my tongue and leave my body in the scream. Some of them are running. I scream. Someone has stopped dead at the sound of my voice. My scream burns into my flesh, and shoots up my spine before bursting into my head, an explosion of terror. Evidence of life.

We are sitting on Nikki's couch. Our friends crowd around us, comforting and hugging us. I feel nothing. I am completely empty. I hear my friend crying and complaining of pain. I feel tears carving a path down my cheeks. I screamed loudly as we were walking back to the house. I screamed, "Make them stop looking at me!" I screamed it over and over and over again until everyone who was still at the party turned away from us.

I saw it in their eyes. I was not Michelle anymore. I was already the girl who got raped. And I hated it. But when I sat down on the couch I stopped. I stopped screaming. I stopped. Everything stopped.

Someone tries to give me water. I push it away. Julia holds me.

"We phoned the cops. They're on their way." She rubs my back.

I glare at her. Is she insane? The last place I want to go now is the police station. I want to go home. *Now.* I want to climb into bed. I am tired. So tired. I want it to be over.

I hope the police don't come.

Every time my friend moves, her face contorts with pain. From down there. I don't feel anything. I stare at her. When they found us, I was convinced that we shouldn't tell anyone we were raped. My plan was to say that we were mugged and return to the party. But the moment our friends came, she started shouting, "We were raped! We were raped!"

I don't understand how she found the words to do that. I don't know how she found a way to tell them.

I take Julia's phone and dial my mom's number. No answer.

All I want is to speak to my mom. I want my mom to come and hold me. I need my mom to tell me everything's okay. That it's not my fault and that she loves me. I need my mom.

The edges of the phone blur. My mom isn't answering. I can't remember my stepdad's cellphone number.

"Is there anything you want? I there anything we can get you?" They all look at me.

"I want my mom." My voice is flat. Lifeless. Words are so much effort.

Malini hugs me. "You are safe now," she says. I believe her. "It's over."

But I don't want them to touch me. I want them to leave me alone. I want everyone to go away. I want my mom. And my bed. That's it.

"Where the fuck are the police?" I hear them shouting outside.

I don't care. I hope they never come. I want to go to bed. I need to sleep.

Someone decides to drive us to the police station. Some of the girls help my friend stand. She grimaces in pain when she rises. I push them away when they try to get near me.

Somewhere during the rape, we lost our shoes. And strangely enough, it is raining outside. It's so surreal; I thought that only happens in movies. Perfect setting, I think, detached from my surroundings, panning out the camera in my head. My feet smack the puddles; I zoom in on my red toenails dirtied with mud. The night is black. The street lamps flicker in our wake, and the roads are deathly quiet, the quiet of a small town soundly sleeping. We walk to the car. Everyone looks at me. I can see it in their eyes.

I am not Michelle. I'm the girl who was raped.

2.

EARLIER THAT DAY

"*A*NY MAN CAN RAPE": *Male Students Talk About Rape.* I squint at the title of my thesis on the PowerPoint presentation as I watch person after person pile into the small room allocated to my presentation. The colloquium is the end-of-year event where the University of Cape Town Psychology Honours students present the research topic they have spent the year working on. I'm scared I may have made use of false advertising. My thesis topic sounds a lot more sensational than I planned. It's just a comment that one of my male participants made, and now the room is packed beyond capacity because everyone thinks I have something interesting to say.

My study examined how rape is socially constructed and socially defined in men's everyday talk. I spoke to ten students (one black, one mixed-race, two Indian, and six white) about three different rape scenarios. The first scenario was about female stranger rape, the second scenario took place in an intimate relationship, and the third scenario was similar to the first scenario but was of male rape. The whole day my fellow students have been either triumphing or getting ripped to shreds in neatly coordinated thirty-minute time slots. At one p.m., I have the second-to-last slot of the day. Despite my knowledge on the topic and all my hard work, I feel unprepared for professional scrutiny.

My mom and stepdad flew up from Port Elizabeth for the occasion. I told them that the colloquium, where I present the first professional research I have ever done, meant more to me than my graduation, where you merely walk across the stage and collect a certificate. I feel proud to show them the windowless, airless room where I spent this year being challenged, moved, angered, and bored by many a lecturer. I love how my mom hugs all of my friends when she is introduced to them instead of shaking their hands.

This is where I belong, with this strangely put-together group of people who think and feel too much, who come from completely different backgrounds, yet share a depth of intellect, hurt, and sarcasm which binds us together in ways we don't always understand. Most people don't study psychology simply because they want to help others. They study psychology because they've been hurt, want to understand that hurt and assist others through that pain.

They stand out like sore thumbs, my doting Afrikaans parents. My tiny mom with her wild hair streaming out in a hundred different directions and her carefully applied red lipstick. My stepdad, Medical Doctor Theunis Christoffel Botha, all dressed up in his wool suit and professional tie. I'm worried that my thesis topic might be a bit scandalous for him. He's a conservative man, and he seems ill at ease with the liberal Psychology department where sex and prostitution are brought up casually over a cup of tea. This is a man who uses "Muis!" as a swear word. But there they stand, undaunted by the crowd, their faces shining with pride—and I haven't even started my presentation yet.

My best friend Ashley strides in and stands with them.

"Friend! I can't believe you came!" I hug her. My blonde house-mate is as tall as Oom Theunis. Her confidence creates a space of intimidation around her. Oom Theunis is oblivious to it.

"I ran over from the hospital, but I wouldn't miss this for the world!" she says. Ashley, a medical student, starts talking to Oom Theunis while my mom and I get a cup of tea.

"You look so happy." She squeezes my hand and beams.

I don't want to let any of them down. I can't believe they are all here for me, to see what I dedicated my year to.

I have a passion for research and what I'm doing. The hours I spent hunched alone in dark rooms, confined to a desk with coffee and backaches, are worth it when I see my mom looking at me with blind trust in my abilities. The tears and self-doubt are forgotten when I realise that my project is worthwhile and the people in my life will support me no matter what.

The three of them sit front row centre and wait for me to speak. My body runs on a combination of adrenaline, caffeine, and cigarettes. I forgot to eat breakfast that morning. The hazy fluorescent bulbs of the room cast a white, hot light on the blue carpet and I feel the cheap material of my "professional" blouse scratching out sweat from my armpits.

I start: "A woman born in South Africa has a greater chance of being raped than learning how to read ..."

I stumble a bit over my words, and my hands shake slightly. I look over the sea of blank faces, reassured by the fact that my mom catches my eye and nods as though I make sense. I have no idea whether sounds are leaving my mouth in comprehensible sentences. My head spins with the certainty that my whole thesis is an unmitigated disaster.

I come to the results section of my study. Here I talk about the interviews I conducted and what my participants said. I specifically interviewed male students and spoke to them about rape because I wanted to understand rape from the male perspective. I was tired of rape being a "woman's problem"—that women have to take responsibility for getting raped and preventing rape. I wanted to know more about how men experience rape. I believed that without the described experiences of the part of society who mostly perpetrates rape, we will never solve the problem. The aim of my thesis was to get a better understanding of how young, modern South African males talk about rape, and whether they perceived rape to be a problem, or something that even affected them at all.

My hands stop shaking. I don't have to look at my notes to know what I have to say anymore. I know this. I've got this. This is my work. This is important. I put down my notes and look into people's eyes as I speak to them. From my heart, about what I believe in.

"Women are made aware by their social surroundings that they live in a dangerous world and that they have to change their behaviour to suit this world."

I walk across the room, and speak with my hands. I think about how each year in Stellenbosch the campus police would come to our residence and tell us how to behave in order not to get raped. It never crossed my mind that there was something wrong with this until I wrote my thesis. Words flow from my mouth.

"Some of the men I interviewed described South Africa as a dangerous country to support the idea that rape is a 'women's problem.' For example, one said: 'Especially in South Africa, you need to be careful. It's a lot harder for a woman to walk around by herself.... It's a much bigger security risk.'

"Another guy said: 'Unfortunately, with our rates of rape in South Africa and crime.... It's an unfortunate product of a corrupted society that one has to be aware of evil.'"

I look one of my female friends in the eyes. Why are we the ones who have to adjust our lives?

"By recognising and accepting the world as a dangerous place, they ignored how rape limits the social spaces that we have access to. They describe rape as an inevitable consequence of living in our 'dangerous society.' Following on this way of thinking, blaming the victim was the knee-jerk reaction of every single one of the men.

"As one man said of the case study: 'The fact that someone was walking behind her and it didn't arouse suspicion, to me that seems, like, a bit naïve.' They described the female victim as 'stupid,' 'foolish,' and 'silly.'

"When people use words like these to describe the rape survivor, it reduces her status as a legitimate rape victim by implying that she triggered her attack through her own carelessness. The responsibility of the rape is removed from the rapist and is placed on the victim. It becomes a case of 'she got herself raped' instead of 'the rapist did this to her.' The rapists' behaviour is 'normalised' and the victim is blamed in a way that seems 'rational'—she should have known better. When victims become the focus of a crime, they also become the target for intervention. Society is preoccupied with changing and controlling 'wayward' females, while the seriousness of rape as a crime is undermined."

It is important to me that everyone realise the truth. We blame the victim because it is convenient. We blame the victim because we think we can rationalise and control his or her behaviour.

It is the comfortable option, thinking that if we can adjust the potential victim's behaviour we can avoid this horrific crime. But, in so doing, we forget the choice that the rapist made. We forget that, no matter what the victim did, the rapist chose to rape.

I go on: "Society also provides a context for rape by setting preconditions of what is acceptable behaviour from both men and women. The 'acceptable' behaviour is defined by patriarchal standards of feminine and masculine qualities—women are passive victims while men are active, strong, and powerful. For example, one man said that, 'Like the guy would go out late at night clubbing or partying and he would be fine, if girls do that maybe on her way home she might get raped.' It was acknowledged that men have an inherent physical power over all women when one of the men I interviewed said, 'Any man can rape.'

"Statements like these reinforce patriarchal notions that depict women as weak objects onto which men can force their strength. Also, the men in my study expressed more shock when referring to a male being raped as opposed to a female being raped: 'It's a bit strange that he is a man and got raped by a man because you should be able to fight him off. I mean, women are obviously, like, less able to do that....'

"Many of the men in the study also used patriarchal notions of what was acceptable behaviour from females in general. Through their talk, it was clear that conservative women deserved more respect while females who act 'inappropriately' (by getting drunk or wearing 'slutty clothing') were met with disgust. It emerged from five of the participants that females had to act according to a set standard of what is acceptable before they could be respected by men."

I hear Ashley snort. Both she and I have been the girls that behave "inappropriately" because we chose to live our lives according to our impulses and have fun. Why are we judged for trying to explore and make sense of our lives in the way we choose?

"In other words, women are socially deviant when they do not follow rules set for them by a patriarchal culture. In this way, they are to blame for men wanting to rape them. A 'Just World' way of thinking comes into play—women are raped because they broke set rules of appropriate feminine behaviour. It assumes that, if the woman didn't break these rules, she wouldn't have been raped.

"While most of the men in my study believed that the rapists are psychopathic strangers, numerous studies have found that most rape victims are raped by someone they know. By insisting that the rapist is an 'unknown, psychopathic other,' the men in the study failed to recognise the role that all men play in supporting a rape-supportive culture in how they talk and act. In this way, they could distance themselves from the act of rape and deny responsibility for all rapes, as they themselves are not deviant, psychopathic individuals."

I think of the rape jokes that my male friends make and how I always force myself to laugh at them because I never want to be the "uncool" girl. I think about how I've labelled other girls as "sluts" because of what they wear and how they act. Why is it that men can act inappropriately and we all just write them off as jerks, while, if a women acts inappropriately, she is breaking some greater societal rule? A drunk man touches your bum in a club: he's an asshole and you move on. A woman wears a short skirt, is drunk, and gets raped: she was asking for it.

"Rape myths promote false accounts of what rape is. They give men unspoken permission to rape and help them rationalise and evade responsibility for sexually violent behaviour. For example, one of the guys in the study described rape as a sex act and not a crime that is about power: 'But power, I don't really, it's not really a big issue, it's not really something that fits here. Rape is just purely arousal.'

"When someone describes rape as only being about sex, it becomes a potentially pleasurable act rather than a crime of violence and oppression. Because of this, the aspect of rape which emphasises the need to conquer and control the victim is ignored.

"Many men defend rape by describing it as a sex act, and sex is something in which the woman can potentially participate. An act of violence, however, reduces the victim to an object onto which power and control is exerted. So by making rape about sex, and not about violence and control, the boundaries of victim participation are blurred."

As my twenty minutes draw to a close, my supervisor jumps up.

"And now for the questions." My stomach drops.

I saw the most severe lecturer in our department, Shane, taking notes throughout my presentation. This is not a good sign.

The first couple of questions are not too hard, I answer them easily enough. Then Shane raises his hand. This is a man who proudly boasts that he once made an entire honours class cry. He also regularly fails the most intelligent students in our class. Once, when I was two minutes late for class, he said that: "Timeliness is next to cleanliness and we all know what cleanliness is next to." This tells you all you need to know about him: he's a man who degrades already sub-par proverbs.

"I want to ask you about your title, 'Any Man Can Rape.' Do you not feel this is a bit misleading?"

I am scared. Perhaps it was misleading. Perhaps I was wrong. Perhaps my whole year was a mistake and I never should have done this research. Then I shake my head. *Stop that*, I scold myself. I worked hard, and I am passionate about this subject, and my results are worthwhile and real. They deserve to be recognised. I push up my sleeves and step forward. I will not let this man undermine this work. My work.

"Well, a lecturer once told me I should have a catchy title," I say as I turn around and pretend to clear my throat.

He was the lecturer who said this to me. Everyone starts sniggering and I hear someone gasp as they catch my sarcasm.

Before I can finish my response, he goes on, "How would you feel if I came out with a title that said '*All Women Should Be Raped?*'"

"Well, that would make me want to attend your presentation and see what it's all about. And here you are, so..." I shrug, as if that about sums up the whole situation.

Before I can go on with my explanation, the whole room erupts in cheers. Someone even whistles. I am startled by their enthusiasm.

When another student states her support in her question, I add that it was never my intention to target men but rather that my title was a quotation from one of my *male* participants, in case anyone couldn't see the quotation marks in my title or didn't hear the explanation of it in my speech. I also didn't bother to go into the semantic differences between the words "can" and "should," because really, none of us is ten years old.

When the questions end, I am euphoric. People run up to me. My hands are full of papers and notes, so my supervisor grabs my shoulder and shakes it.

"Congratulations!" he repeats over and over again. He smiles and his little face crinkles with pride. I introduce Professor Hardy to my parents, and they chat about my work. I can see my mom is overwhelmed with emotion and on the verge of crying. Oom Theunis grabs me in a stiff, uncomfortable hug.

"That was amazing!" Amala says.

"Dude, oh my gosh, do you even realise what you just did?" Malini says.

I laugh.

"When you pushed up your sleeves, I knew that man was in trouble," my mom says.

"I can't believe that just happened," I say.

My stepdad's chest is puffed up like some kind of bird. He's talking to my supervisor about my future, my career, and my "potential."

"Where did Shane go?" I ask my mom.

"He ran out as soon as it was over, I think he was so ashamed." My mom looks worried about him. She's obviously never met the man.

"I didn't know you had it in you," Nick says to me later, when I sit in front of him. I don't blame him. People usually don't.

As we sit around and chat, everyone talks about my presentation. I am officially an intellectual bad-ass. I get a message from Ashley.

"Friend, sorry I had to run, I was late. But as I left, one of your classmates also ran out, and he was saying, 'presentation of the year!' I concur. You are simply amazing, and I am blown away. Wow."

3.

AFTER OUR FRIENDS FOUND US, they phoned the police at twelve-thirty a.m. I got home at nine the next morning. In those eight hours, what the rape had not shattered was destroyed by the way the police and the hospital treated us. The rape robbed us of our physical security and trust in men. The police and the hospital robbed us of our basic human dignity. The institutions that were supposed to start putting the pieces back together broke us even further. We were no longer people. We were the girls who were stupid enough to get raped. And we were treated as such.

Every bone in my body is frozen. But I'm not cold.

As we are getting into the car the police van arrives. Two fat men get out.

"Who are the rape victims?"

Julia points to my friend and me. The officers look at us. Pause. They seem skeptical. What, do I not look like I was raped enough?

"We will take you to the station and start the proper procedure," says Number One.

"These girls need immediate medical attention. What are your measures with regards to this?" Julia's formerly white-and-pink outfit is now white, pink, and brown. The mud and dirt of the evening is splattered all over her. She squares off against the two officers even though she barely reaches their shoulders.

"We take them to the police station and from there, to the hospital."

She doesn't blink. "Because medical treatment should be the first priority right now."

"We have all the proper procedures at the police station, they will get medical treatment." Number One is irritated by the Power Ranger's know-it-all attitude. Number Two doesn't speak.

"Okay," she relents.

"Don't leave me," I tell Julia. There is no way that I am getting into a car with two strange men. It doesn't matter that they are the police. In fact, the uniform scares me. It seems sinister.

Julia, Malini, my friend, and I drive to the police station in the police car. No one talks. We look at the rain obscuring the lights, causing them to flicker and hurt our eyes. We should be safe. Four of us against the two of them. We should be safe enough.

It is the first time I think this way.

At the police station, we are put in a bare room with wooden floors, one round table, and chairs for us to sit on. I start to feel cold. Chills run up and down and through my body. I am glad my friends are here. I am aware of them talking. I make a joke at one point. I shiver.

"Mich."

I look at Julia.

"Don't block this out." Julia is a qualified social worker and used to counsel at a Rape Crisis clinic. She knows. "I know it is the easiest thing in the world, but don't block it out."

As I look into her brown eyes, I feel it. I feel everything. I feel my tears, I feel shock, I feel scared, I feel death, I feel hopeless and I feel broken.

I put my head in my hands. That's when I smell him. He is still on my hands. His sex is sticky against my fingers.

"Shit ... I smell him," I look at Julia. There's nothing we can do. I'm not allowed to wash my hands.

She rubs my back. "It's so ironic."

"My thesis," I say.

We look at each other.

A female police officer comes in. I have to make an official statement.

I am tired. I want to sleep.

She leads me to another cold, empty room with a big table and plastic chairs. They are all empty, except for the two we sit on.

The statement takes an hour and a half to make. I think the idea is that they send a female police officer to female rape victims to make them feel more comfortable. For all the emotional support she gave me, I would have felt more comfortable with a wooden plank. First I have to tell her exactly what happened, the whole story in precise detail. It is the first time I tell it to anyone. No response. She doesn't even blink. Her empty face plants seeds of doubt in my mind. Then I have to tell her again. This time she writes it down. She can't spell, and I have to help her with some of words.

"D-r-a-g-g-e-d," I spell. I don't correct her when I see her write down "draged."

"And then we lay—"

"No!" She interrupts.

"Sorry?" I whisper.

"You only know what happens to you," she tells me.

Okay.

"And then I lay there," I say.

I am so tired. My brain is thick and foggy, and I struggle to put sentences together. Words jump around in my head and get lost on their way to my mouth. My arm takes forever to move across the table. To sign my statement. They ask me if I will recognise him. I don't know.

They move me to the "comfort room." No, seriously, it's called the "comfort room." For people who are in distress. My friend, Malini, and Julia are already there. My friend makes her statement. They don't take her to another room; she gets to do it with us there. In the "comfort room," bright colours jump out at me. There are pictures and paintings. A carpet. And sofas. I sit in a single armchair so that no one can sit next to me.

Where is my mom? I want my mom.

An elderly lady is sitting opposite me and looks at me tenderly. The resident counsellor. "Do you want to tell me what happened?"

Are you kidding me? "No."

She starts small talk to distract me. I guess no one told her we are psychology students. I stop being able to handle her questions when she asks me what the weather is like in Canada, where my dad lives. I tell her I'm cold, and she gives me a blanket. I pretend to sleep. Mostly for her protection.

"Sleep is a great healer," she peers at Julia over her rimmed glasses.

I imagine smashing her head against the table so that she will shut up.

"Then they dragged us..." My friend is re-telling what happened.

The same words I used.

Click, click, click. High heels walking down the passage.

My mom! I start to let everything go. This can only end when she comes. The door opens. I don't have to be strong anymore.

A police officer comes in.

My mom still isn't answering her phone. For some reason I remember the address of my uncle in Durbanville. I give that to the police and hope that they will reach my mom and my stepdad.

We wait.

A detective comes and tells us it's time to go to the hospital. It's three a.m. The four of us walk back into the rain. I am so cold. I am so tired. Julia is still wearing her pink Power Ranger outfit, and she is bossing the detective around, telling him what to do and how. The detective is wearing plainclothes and has curly hair. He doesn't look either my friend or me in the eye.

We drive to the hospital. There are four of us, so hopefully we are safe with this man. He doesn't talk. I can't get a read on him. He is handsome, late thirties, unbothered and unencumbered by what happened to us. I get a whiff of irritation. He thinks we are useless.

When we arrive at the hospital he tells the man at reception, "I have two rape survivors with me. They need to have rape kits administered to them."

I realise I already hate that word—"survivor." It is not what he thinks of us. It's what they told him to call us. At some workshop where they served cold coffee and tuna mayo sarmies, they told him to refer to us as "rape survivors." And he does, not because he believes it, but because it is part of the "proper procedure."

My friend is outside on the phone. She is telling her parents what happened. Julia is with her. Malini takes my hand, and we wait in yet another room—the nurses' station. Malini's wild hair is curling with the rage and emotions I know she is doing her best to keep inside. People run around and through us; I watch them moving through a thick fog. I sit on a plastic chair and wait. Malini stands guard. My eyes won't open.

Two nurses work at a table with their backs turned to us. They have yet to acknowledge we exist. The detective goes to them.

"Hey auntie," he smiles at the nurse, and his tone is playful.

"Wat het jy nou vir ons?" The nurse is curt, unresponsive to his flirting. She wants to know what he has for them.

They carry on speaking in Afrikaans. They don't know that I can speak Afrikaans.

"Two students who were raped. They were at the beach, they were partying. You know how it is." The teasing tone never leaves his voice. They have their backs to us.

"What are they? Stupid? They know what the world is like!" The nurse is mad. At us. The "rape survivors." I feel anger pushing and rushing about inside of me.

"Listen," I say, in Afrikaans, to their backs, "if you have something to say about what happened to me tonight, please do it to my face."

Neither the detective nor the nurse turns around.

"Ja, I will," the nurse says. She does not turn around. "What were you thinking? You know what the world is like!"

I can't speak. I can't feel. It was my fault. It was my fault. She just said so.

"Listen here, my friend really does not need to hear this right now so will you please just shut up," Malini sneers at the nurse's back. She squeezes my hand.

They shut up. But now I know. Because strangers won't lie to protect you.

It is my fault. I deserved this. I had it coming. I am broken, and it is my fault. I know better than to think like this but I am so tired. And the people who are supposed to help me just confirmed it. The people our government pays to help "rape survivors" just told me the truth.

No matter what the theories and my feminist principles say: It's my fault that I got raped.

Is this really happening?

A different nurse tells me to go to the bathroom and pee in the cup. I leave the room without looking at the nurse or the detective, Malini behind me.

I pee in the cup, my warm piss spilling over my sticky hands, running onto my sleeves. In the hall on the way back to the nurses' room, I collapse. Everything inside of me is done. It's all gone. Like a helpless cow, caught in barbed wire, I struggle for life and air but I'm defeated. I am blind with pain, and I'm no longer me. Tears, tears, so many tears.

"Aaaaaaaaaah," I moan and rock my body. Snot, spit, piss, sticky sex, and tears. That is who I am now.

"Is it my ... fault? Did ... I do ... this?" I heave. Malini grabs me and holds onto me.

In the distance, I see the detective walking down the corridor in our direction. His expression doesn't change when he sees me lying on the floor. He turns into the room.

"Malini!" I am hysterical. Lost. Out of control. "It's ... my ... fault!"

"Mich, no!" Malini holds me. "None of this is your fault! You cannot blame yourself!"

I am glad that she is there. But I don't believe her. I gather myself. Again. And I push myself up. Again.

"It's going to feel like you are being raped again," Julia says to me before they administer the rape kit. I still haven't been able to wash myself or drink anything since I was raped. It is now about five-thirty a.m.

I go first. The doctor is a young female. The purple circles under her eyes are pronounced despite her thick, smeared glasses. She is thin and has dark stains on her scrubs. She asks me what happened. I tell her.

"Well, at least nothing else happened. You know, you weren't stabbed or anything."

I get it. I was "just" raped. Fabulous. Yay me.

I take off all of my clothes and put them into a plastic bag. "I'm on my period," I realise. How did I forget about it?

"Are you wearing a tampon?"

I nod.

"Take it out and give it to me."

Naked, I dig inside myself for my tampon. I am cold and dry. I move my fingers, digging deeper. Finally, I find the tampon. I wrench it out.

"Oh, that is so good! Lots of DNA evidence there!" The doctor folds my tampon away.

I comb through my hair. Yank strands out. She swabs my nails. She cuts my nails. She swabs my cheek where he licked it. She pricks my finger for an HIV test. She decides it is an appropriate time to speak.

"You know, a lot of doctors struggle with bedside manner. I, however, was really sick as a child and spent a lot of time in hospitals." She plucks a pubic hair. "This made me better able to empathise with people, and while it was hard being sick so often, I do believe it has made me a better doctor."

It's like they're hitting me over and over again with a cartoon anvil.

"Well, my parents got divorced when I was nine because my dad went bankrupt," I tell her. "My sister died in a car crash when I was fifteen, and when I was nineteen, another guy forced himself on me while I was drunk. I also have clinical depression. So yes, I do get that bad things happen. I just kind of thought that I had reached my quota for a while," I say in one breath.

She shuts up.

And hands me a silver tray with colourful pills to fight against what he put inside of me.

I drink a pill to kill what might have been a baby.

A pill for the sexually transmitted diseases he might have given me.

Another pill.

Another one.

These two might be the anti-retrovirals.

I don't ask.

They stick in my throat.

I lie down and spread my legs. Nurses walk in and out of the room without knocking.

She doesn't warn me before she puts the cold, metal cylinder inside of me. I look into the blinding light. She doesn't warn me before she cracks it open and breaks me in half. It hurts. It hurts so much. The world swims in front of me. While breaking me, she swabs my womb. Red DNA.

I walk out of the room, wearing only a thin hospital gown with an open back. The wind floats up my legs and exposes me.

"Your mom is here," Julia tells me as I walk into the hospital "comfort room."

There are fucking comfort rooms everywhere.

"Where?" As I ask, my mom runs into the room. Finally.

I fall into the safest place into the world, her arms.

My mom sobs as she hugs me.

I pull away from her and look into her eyes. "Mom, I need you to stop crying right now," I tell her as nicely as I can. I watch her pull herself together.

"Okay," she nods. Her small, knobby fingers wipe her tears away.

She is in control. And that's when I am safe again.

I sit in the car and wait for Ashley and Jessica, my housemates. My stepdad sits next to me. While he was driving me home, we got lost, and even though I knew he was going in the wrong direction, I let him figure out how to get to my house without bossing him around.

The night before, I sent both Ashley and Jessica a Facebook message telling them I was raped. When my stepdad and I arrived home, they weren't there. I didn't know it then, but Jessica woke up at six a.m. and, for some reason, decided to check her Facebook messages. When she read my message, she woke Ashley and together they phoned every hospital in the Muizenburg area to look for me. Ashley's a fifth year medicine student and she knows what happens to "rape survivors." They packed a bag of comfortable clothes for me with my pills, and everything else they could think that I would need, including chocolate. When my stepdad and I reached our house, they were God knows where, taking on the world in their epic search for me. Later, Ashley told me that she had her textbook open on her lap, reading up on rape kits while Jessica was driving. She also took her student card in case she had to force her way into a ward.

Unfortunately, their heroic mission was cut short as I was already at our front door, and my keys had been taken along with all my other things the night before. My mom was still at the hospital. I left her holding my friend's hand as she was getting her rape kit administered. I just wanted to get into bed.

When Jessica's Yaris pulls up, I get out of my stepdad's car but can't look my best friends in the eye. I am barefoot on the wet pavement, my stepdad's grey knitted jersey thrown over my blue hospital gown. My black hair is wild and my eyes dull. Jessica comes over and wraps her arms around me. I harden myself against her. I look over her shoulder. I see Ashley and my stepdad holding each other next to his rental car. He's crying with absolute abandon in her arms, like he's the child and she's the adult.

I turn around and walk inside our little student house in Claremont. In my room, Ashley and Jessica take off my jersey and the blue hospital gown. Usually bashful, I barely notice that I am naked in front of them. Ashley starts to fold the blue hospital gown.

"Throw it away," I tell her.

They help me step into the shower. I know I'm dirty but the desire that overwhelms me is to sleep—my awareness of being dirty or sore is secondary. The only reason I shower is because I don't want to wake up smelling him on me.

Sleep is the sweetest release, safest escape, the shadow of comfort that hides me from my new reality where I am a stranger to myself. I sleep for twelve hours, but it is not a continuous sleep. My mind is able to slip into a black hole of exhaustion, wiping out rape and everything associated with it, but my body is not convinced that I am safe.

The most horrible experience is waking up.

Sleep allows me to forget; to become nothing but a floating entity that has no identity, history, or memories. But then I have to wake up and remember what I am now. My eyes start to flutter, and I feel the physical memory of *it* poisoning my stomach—before I can mentally remember *it*. My body is drenched in the nausea of foreboding, the sickness of almost remembering. And then it comes. The knowledge of what I now am. And the nightmare is being awake. The punishment is consciousness. As I sleep, I am vaguely aware of Jessica coming in and bringing me water and coming again a while later to put down some snacks on my bedside table.

I start. This time I'm scared. I move each of my shaky limbs out of my bed and walk into the lounge. Ashley and Jessica are sitting on the couches.

"Hey," I say.

"Hey," they chorus, concerned. I can see they don't know what to say.

"Where's my mom?"

"She went shopping."

I feel betrayed. Where else should my mother be except with me? They take me back to my bed, and I tell them what happened. It's the fourth time that I've told the story and it's only been twelve hours since it's happened. When I tell them about how I couldn't get his penis in, Ashley gets mad.

"That's pathetic, I mean, if he is going to go through the effort of raping you he might as well do it properly!" We smile at each other, and I realise that she sees me. Not rape.

Jessica sits on my desk chair and watches me, folding her little body into my desk chair, as I fall asleep again.

That evening my mom and stepdad come. They have bought me a brand-new camera so that I can "move on with my life." My mom is already trying to fix me and I haven't even registered that I'm broken yet. I eat some meat from a braai they had gone to but the sickness won't leave my stomach. My mom, my stepdad, and I all sit on my bed.

There's a knock on my door.

"Your friend's in the hospital," Ashley says.

"What?"

"She's bleeding excessively but she's stable. Malini is with her and her parents are on their way down."

I hear this but it doesn't settle down in my mind. Ashley, Jessica, my mom and stepdad talk for a bit. My stepdad leaves and tells me he's going back to Port Elizabeth the next day. My mom is staying until the end of the week.

That night my mom wraps her tiny body around mine and holds me so fiercely that even my nightmares stay away.

4.

WHEN I WAKE UP THE NEXT MORNING, my thighs, back and buttocks are a sickly greenish purple from where they kicked me, dragged me, and threw me on the rocks. Every muscle in my body aches. My hands are completely numb and tinged blue from when I struggled in panic with the shoelaces. Surprisingly, my face is fine. I was right, the one who punched me didn't hit that hard. But my vagina is tender. It hurts to pee but I'm not bleeding.

I pick up my foundation, and slowly smear it across my nose, cheeks, and forehead. I rub it in. My skin looks smooth, blemish-free. I apply some mascara. No one who looks at me today will be able to tell. Outside, the sky is grey.

The night before my mom and stepdad brought back my keys, my wallet with my driver's license, and all of my cards.

"How?" I ask.

"Your classmates. They found your stuff and your friend's stuff. They gave it to us when we went back to fetch your car."

At the thought of them on the rocks in search of pieces of my friend and me, sharp fists punch my stomach. How long did it take them?

How many people know how broken I am?

I pack my wallet in my handbag.

My mom and I go to the V&A Waterfront to replace some of the stuff that was stolen, like my cellphone and my watch. Why? It was the only thing we could think of doing. Unlike when someone dies, there was no funeral to plan, no condolences to receive. Unlike a physical injury, there was no resting to heal. I couldn't stay in bed the whole day—it felt too much like giving up. I look at a watch and remember something.

"Nick found me," I tell my mom. "I think everyone was scared to touch me because of how I was screaming, but I couldn't move, you know, because of the shoelaces, so he untied the ones around my ankles. That's when I knew I wouldn't die. My jeans were still undone and everyone was watching me and while they were watching I had to zip up my fly and do the top button."

She listens and lets me talk, without interrupting or crying or getting angry. I wonder if this is how she listens to her clients. She is a psychologist. The whole day and for many days afterwards little vomits of that night come up, and she takes them from me and packs them away.

Malini messages my mom and tells her that my friend is okay. I forgot that she was in the hospital. How?

We spend money. Necklaces, rings, a watch. I don't want a cellphone. I don't want to talk. What the rapists didn't take the police did—my favourite denim jacket and black jeans. Also purple lacy underwear that now feel wrong. Everything I thought I knew about rape and rape theories in principal is a little harder to put into practice now that I am a "survivor."

I am still scared. Everything about me is less. I feel physically smaller than I did two days ago. My breath is shallow, and you can see right through me if you try.

In Woolworths' dairy aisle I am sending a message to one of my best friends, Mackenzie, from my mom's phone when I see another message from one of our family friends.

"We are thinking of you during this time. X"

My stomach contracts. Black and grey spots cover the white floor. Bile rises in my throat. I can't move.

People can't know. It's my fault. People can't know. It's my fault. People can't know.

I'm dirty now.

I walk to my mom who's picking up a container of strawberry yoghurt—the kind with little pieces of fruit in it.

"You ... can't ... TELL PEOPLE!" I yell.

She looks at me. What she sees scares her.

I shove the phone at her.

"She knows," I implore. Clouds of panic in my eyes. "She knows! This is my story. I decide who knows. No one else. Me."

"Okay. I understand."

"It's not happening to them. I decide who knows."

"Should I ask everyone not to tell anyone?"

"Yes!" Can't she see it? How dirty I am? Why doesn't she understand? "This happened to me, they don't have the right to … talk."

I can't breathe.

"Okay, I'm messaging her right now. See? I'm doing it right now." She taps on her phone with her one hand while her other hand rubs circles on my back. "I'll tell everyone that you are taking control. You will decide when and where you want to talk about it, okay?"

Okay.

That night Mackenzie comes over. We sit on the front porch of our house in Claremont, looking at the leafy suburban streets while I tell her what happened. She is angry.

Inside, I hear the comforting clatter of pots as my mom cooks dinner. Ashley, Jessica, Mackenzie, and I are all friends from high school in Port Elizabeth.

On the wooden table in the dining room, Ashley lays a white tablecloth. A pot of my mom's mince pasta is on it, and we sit obediently as my mom dishes for us. Once she's done with a plate, she adds a sprig of coriander—for flavour. I sink my toes deep into the cream carpet and sip the red wine, which is much easier to swallow than the food.

Although we don't speak much about the rape, it is there, an ever-present shadow, showing itself every time one of us gets up, moves our hands, shakes our head. But, instead of being scared of the shadow, we welcome it, and drink with it, embrace it. That night we choose to celebrate the little love that is left in me and not the hate that someone else planted. We manage to laugh as well.

I look at the small lines which run and swerve and collide across my mom's face. And the deeper ones around her eyes, which sometimes catch her tears before letting them fall.

"Michelle," my mom says.

"What?"

"What were you thinking? Trying to hit him with a panga?" Her mouth easily breaks open into a laugh as she talks, "You can't even walk across a flat surface without tripping!" She claps her hands once—loudly—as her body rocks forward.

I shake my head. Sure mom, *now's* the time to talk about how clumsy I am; but I feel a smile sneaking into the corner of my mouth, and once that happens, we all laugh for a long time.

The next day, I look out of a window at a green Stellenbosch suburban garden where a Jack Russell and a black Labrador chase each other. I have looked at this garden probably a hundred times before while experiencing a thousand different emotions. I'm at my therapist's office, Dr. Adriaanse. As an undergraduate student at Stellenbosch, I was clinically depressed and alone. I was studying Politics, Philosophy, and Economics but was unsure of what I wanted to do with it in the future. I felt like I didn't fit in with my friends; I was an outsider. I had also never dealt with the death of my sister, Roneldi. All this led to a very unhappy me who landed in a heap in front of Dr. Adriaanse in the middle of my third year. Together we slay my depression, with the help of some very strong pills.

I had stopped seeing him though. I was happy this past year. I liked living in Cape Town, studying what I loved, surrounded by people I fit in with, in a city of cultural and spiritual diversity. And now I'm back. Sitting in the same antique chair with wooden swirls for handles and stiff stuffing, splitting open slightly on the right side. Dr. Adriaanse sits in a twin chair and in between us is a small wooden coffee table whose sole purpose is to offer a box of tissues to me.

Dr. Adriaanse looks upset. His grey hair is disheveled, and his face is drawn.

"My dear, dear friend. I am so ... angry," he purses his lips together. Taught to maintain professional boundaries with patients and to stay completely neutral, it takes a lot for Dr. Adriaanse to make statements like this.

I tell him The Story of The Rape. It has a life of its own by now and I tell it without feeling anything. In between he mutters things like "monsters" and "can't believe it."

"I'm glad you did that," he says a while after I finish.

"What?"

"Disassociated yourself from what was happening."

"When did I do that?"

"When you were telling yourself not to be there, you were protecting yourself."

Going into a dissociative state during trauma is common. If you are in a situation that's completely beyond your control and you know there's no escape, the only form of self-defence may be to shut down completely. You fight back, not by taking action, but by altering your state of mind. You may still be aware of what is happening, but you are so detached its meaning does not register. In *Trauma Narratives and Herstory*, Silvia Pellicer-Ortin calls this dissociative state "one of nature's small mercies, a protection against unbearable pain." The physical factors behind these different states of minds are unknown.

"Michelle, ever since I received your email I have been thinking about you. And I want you to remember that this ... this is not an obstacle," he pauses. "It is simply a continuation of heroism. All of it. When you took that panga and bang!" he slaps his hand down on his knee, "Even that is evidence that this is simply a continuation of your heroism."

After I've told him everything, he gets up and walks to the bookshelf behind his chair, picks one out and places it in my hands. It's called *Trauma and Recovery* by Judith Lewis Herman.

Ah Judith. She will become a close friend of mine over the next couple of months.

Once the session is over, my mom comes in and the three of us sit down.

"Colleague, I need you to remember to create a safe environment for Michelle right now," he says as he grips my mom's hands tightly. He always calls her "colleague" even though they have only met once before. Before we leave, he asks if he can hug me. His stiff body presses against mine. It's the first time we hug. It feels safe.

The feeling that overwhelms me for the next couple of days is numbness. Sure, I have moments of devastating clarity, where the full force of what happened knocks me down and I can scarcely breathe. I'm not in denial but rather in survivor mode. Being numb means being able to heal myself. The ordinary response to a tragedy is to exile it from your mind, and in those first couple of days I am still hoping that I will wake up and it will all be a bad dream. I feel that, if I tried hard enough, if I was good enough somehow, it will go away and I will be clean again.

My mom leaves at the end of the week. I am handed over to the next caretaker in line: my sister, Janah, flies over from Johannesburg to stay with me for the weekend.

As she strides towards us at the airport, I can feel her eyes searching me, trying to gauge how she should act. Her long, skinny hair whips back and forth across her small, compact body. She's wearing a bright red woollen dress—vintage—and leather boots. Her face is clean but her eyebrows are drawn on, and on her mouth are two perfect red lines, little pieces of which sometimes sit on her teeth when she talks. She's a couple of inches taller than my mom, and a whole lot shorter than me.

Janah tentatively reaches up to kiss me and I feel the invisible thread of camaraderie between us slip back into place. Her pale, bony hands grip my arm fiercely. On her middle finger is a gold ring made of intertwined skulls.

Janah lives in Jo'burg with George, her fiancé. They moved there about a year ago for work: they're both lawyers. She's the reason I left Port Elizabeth to study at Stellenbosch; she was in her fifth year at the university when I started.

She lived in a flat with two of her best friends. During my first year, she would pick me up from my residence, Serruria, and take me to her place, where we would drink too much wine and look at the few flickering lights the city had to offer. I would tell her about my experiences. How excited I was about being chosen as a cheerleader for our first year Carnival, how sad I was to leave my friends in Port Elizabeth, the way the leaves crunched as I stepped on them on the way to class and the way my breath caught in my throat whenever the man I liked looked at me.

I remember her telling my mom about my first year at varsity: "It's so interesting so see Michelle going through everything I went through. She feels everything very intensely."

With my sister, I tentatively step back into the world. We go to Addis on Cape, an Ethiopian restaurant on the corner of Long and Church Streets, where I drink a glass of wine. We scoop up lentils, spicy beans, and chicken with injera, our hands dripping with sauce.

"How are you Shelletjie?" she asks me.

"I don't know."

I ask her about her life. Whenever Janah drinks a few too many glasses of wine, she becomes confrontational. It's one of the things I like most about her—she doesn't have time for small talk. Despite our religious step-family, Janah has always been an atheist. She asks me why I don't blame God for what happened to me.

I don't know how to answer her. He wasn't there while I was being raped, but I can't think about what that means yet.

I walk with her to the car in the dark after dinner. She grips my hand tightly with her cold fingers.

When we shop on Long Street, I realise I have developed a sixth sense. I notice the way we walk, who walks in front of us and behind us. I notice the dark spaces and shadows, even during the day. I notice the way someone's clothing bulges, just a little, maybe indicating a concealed weapon.

I notice the way a man's footsteps thud behind me. How they become louder and louder until I can hear the wet rag of his breath and smell the sharpness of his sweat. I press my body against the wall and let him pass. The steady thuds don't slow down as he slides past, but as he walks, his eyes, just for an instant, flicker up and down my body.

He's gone but I can't switch off this awareness of everything that happens around me. It exhausts me. I learn later that 'hyper-arousal' is the first, cardinal symptom of Post Traumatic Stress Disorder. After experiencing something traumatic, our bodies go into a state of being permanently alert, as if the danger could return at any moment. Unlike most people whose emotional baseline is a state of relaxation, a trauma victim's body is on a constant hunt for danger, never resting or settling down.

So, the next day my sister and I stay at home. We climb into my bed and wear tights and woolly socks. We eat chocolate and make mushroom burgers. I watch her pale skin and her freckles. I look at her sharp nose. I listen to her breathing, and it doesn't scare me.

A serious issue to address for the modern-age trauma victim is how to re-enter the world of social media. Given how many of the Psych Honours students were at the party, I now had no idea who in my life knew and who didn't know that I was raped. Like an invisible virus, my rape had spread, and I had no idea who it had touched. The problem was how to subtly and appropriately re-introduce myself to Facebook? Or do I just avoid social media forever? I wasn't the kind of person who could just pretend nothing had happened but I also didn't think I could be like, "How about those anti-retrovirals?"

Conundrum.

When I finally sit down, cross-legged on my bed and log onto Facebook, I see the revered red notification which shows me that I have two messages in my inbox. For a moment I'm scared. But I didn't have to be.

Julia: I am so proud of you, and I also believe you are going to be fine in the end because you have the character to take from it and grow! words cannot describe how much I love you, I realised this on friday. It's so strange, I feel heartbroken and angry at the same time. It feels like by raping you they raped me and all the women that I loved at the same time. This has been a hectic process, but you will come through it. and what will come out of this is a group of women who are stronger for it, have a new perception of life, and love each other for the rest of our lives. And no one can take that away from us. You are so brave mich.

Malini: The strength that you showed is something that I will admire forever. No matter how amazing and brave I thought you were before, you've completely surpassed that. You don't know the amount of anger and hatred I felt that evening. I was only able to keep it together because of you. You're something special friend, and there was no place that I would've rather been that evening.

A couple of days after I was raped, a song by Florence + The Machine, "Shake It Out," was released. The first time I heard it I knew it was going to be my "theme song" (I may have watched too much *Ally McBeal* as a teenager). In the song, Florence's voice starts with a melancholic ache, and it slowly builds into a shout. She sings about darkness coming for her and being able to keep it at bay by shaking it off. I dance to it in my room, jumping up and down, arms waving about with abandon, roaring at the devil to get the fuck out. Florence said it in a slightly nicer way. But my lyrics *felt* way better. At the end there's this part where she kind of howls like a sexy wolf, and I was totally into trying to do that.

I made the song's lyrics my first Facebook update.

5.

"CAN YOU FUCKING KEEP FUCKING QUIET please?" Our TESOL instructor, David, yells at us. Somehow, when I first saw him—round, red hair, and gay—I thought he would be fun. He certainly thinks he is. He does things like smoke two cigarettes at once, "secretly" manipulate us, talk about how expensive his manicures are, and ask us about our virginal status.

Some enjoy him more than others.

Janah left a few days ago. I spoke to my mom, and we decided that instead of going back home to Port Elizabeth I'm going ahead with what Malini and I had planned to do, taking a Teaching English to Students of Other Languages (TESOL) class so that we can travel and teach English next year. I want to take a year off from Psychology to go to South Korea.

The TESOL building is in Claremont, in Main Street, a busy area. The students are all foreign. They come from Angola, the DRC, Sudan, Ethiopia, and places in Europe. Most want to improve their English so they can get a job in South Africa, others' parents sent them over to learn English before starting school, while the rest want to improve their English and meet people while on holiday.

Every night we have to teach a lesson. I can't really say if I'm enjoying it or not. Mostly it's nice to get out of the house and learn something new. It means that there are a couple of hours every day that I don't have to think about rape. I like meeting new people who don't know about the rape and don't have "rape eyes." We talk about adventure and travel and grabbing life by the proverbial balls.

Our lecturer keeps on telling us that, while teaching, we should be a cross between "Barney and Hitler." Five months after completing the course we will all receive an email stating that David is no longer associated with the TESOL institution in any way and that we are under no circumstances to send him money. None of us will be surprised.

I give Malini a lift home from class every evening as she doesn't have a car. When we drive home the Thursday night of the first week of the two-week course, she says something strange.

"Do you know what Kate said to me tonight?" Malini and Kate are two of the few non-smokers who stay in class while the rest of us go outside to puff. Kate is a "woe is me" punk girl with tattoos of parrots, a shaved head, and a septum piercing.

"No, what?"

"She said nothing bad has probably ever happened to you."

"What? Why?"

"Because you look like one of those cheerful, happy people that nothing horrible ever happens to."

I don't know how to respond to this. I try to keep my eyes on the road as we drive past Newlands Stadium down Main Street. My hands smoothly change my gears. When I was thirteen years old I saved up to buy a cellphone. It actually looked like a telephone—bulky with a little antenna on the top right hand corner. It had two rubber covers—a luminous yellow one and a bright orange one—which I alternated. The first night I got my phone, I typed in messages to my best friend. We typed for hours, sharing our day since school ended (she did not do her homework), what our dreams were (to become Britney Spears), and talking about our feelings. She sent me a message to say her parents were fighting. My thumbs hesitated. And then they typed. About how much I hated my life. How much I hated myself. About how I once took a piece of broken glass and pressed it into my wrist until bright red drops popped out.

She didn't reply. So I never mentioned it again. The next day we smiled and laughed.

"What did you say to her?"

"I told her she has no idea what she's talking about."

Malini opens the car door and gets out. I watch her walk

across the pavement to her house, the street lamp settling on her soft curls.

At the TESOL classes I am surrounded by men. My body reacts strongly to them. I try to control it or ignore it but I can't. It's been two weeks since I was raped, and I am in enclosed spaces with twenty or more men. I don't always handle it well.

One evening, Malini and I are teaching a group class with Hoi, a Korean in his late teens, who loves teaching so much that he will even teach our lessons, and Bianca, a government travel agent who wants to use her TESOL certificate to travel to South Korea to find a husband.

Michael is a student who always arrives five minutes early for our class. Every day he wears the same red tie and an egg-coloured dress shirt that used to be white. He's clean-shaven and his hair is neatly trimmed. He does his homework, never chats to others while we are teaching, and has insightful questions. We are all madly in-teacher-love with him.

I teach the class prepositions in my over-confident style. I have really taken to the position of power that comes with being called "Teacher." To me, they might as well have been saying "Professor" or "Maestro" or, you know, "The Speaker of All Wisdom."

When I'm done, Hoi teaches. And he goes on. And on. He teaches in a Korean accent that's difficult to make sense of, and by the time Bianca, frowning, begins to teach, most of the class is asleep.

"Why yous look so sad?" she shouts at them and throws her papers on the desk. "Smile, dammit!"

During group work, Michael puts up his hand for me to come help him. I walk to him and lean over his shoulder.

They smell the same.

"Teacher?" I hear Michael call after me but I walk straight out of the room to the bathroom. I know Michael isn't the rapist. He has fine features. And he can't speak Afrikaans—he can barely speak English. But they smell the same. I rub soap around my nostrils to get rid of the smell. I breathe. In and out. In and out.

Back in the classroom, everything's calm. At the end of the class, Michael comes to me: "Teacher, thank you, I now understand everything about preposition. Thanks to you."

I shake his warm, steady hand and look into his clear eyes, "It's my pleasure Michael."

Telling everyone you know that you were raped becomes harder each time. When you are raped, you carry the story inside of you, and there isn't an appropriate time or place or way to announce it. I feel like every single time I told someone I did it wrong. I've done it in person, over Facebook, over email, asked someone else to do it for me, asked someone to come over for a serious talk and then did it. Honestly, all the ways of telling people you were raped overwhelmingly suck ass.

The first couple of weeks after the rape I still didn't want people to know. I Facebooked most people I knew and told them that I was mugged. Then I Facebooked two close friends to tell them that I was raped. One of them, Kelly, told me she would be coming over to visit me one evening after I was finished teaching.

I wake up on the morning of her visit with a headache. By the afternoon, it feels as though someone is punching staples into my scalp and I am constantly heading to the bathroom to dry-heave over the toilet. Physically, I can't handle knowing that I have to talk to someone and explain what happened again. I feel like my body is rejecting the notion, and words jumble around me as my leg jumps and jitters.

When I finally make it home, I climb into the cold sheets and fall asleep.

Before I even open my eyes, I can hear Kelly and Ashley in the kitchen. I lie in my sweat for a while, my body stuck to the bed.

Their footsteps thud towards the couch where I hear cups being put down and big slurps of tea.

I roll around and heave my leg over the bed.

"Wahahahahaha!"

My heart stops.

"That's so funny friend!"

I touch my arm. *Am I really here?*

"It was so insane!" Ashley exclaims.

My breath explodes out of my nostrils in short bursts. Every part of me is on fire.

"*Wahahahahahahahaha!*"

Each laugh is like a stab to my chest. And I lie there, while their laughter boils inside of me, until I am so filled with its bitter taste that I cannot stand it anymore.

I get up and open my door. I storm past them. In the kitchen, I bang around dishes with no purpose other than to make my dissatisfaction known. They come up behind me, and Ashley tries to give me a hug.

"Don't touch me!" I scream.

They stop and look at me in shock. Ashley reaches out to touch me. I shrug her off and take Kelly to my room to talk about what happened. Later I tell them I was upset because I wanted to join them and chat but I couldn't.

We all know I'm lying.

The Clinical Psychology syllabus of our honours degree was taught by Professor Daniels. Her speciality is Gender Psychology. Professor Daniels is skinny, wears loose-fitting grey skirt suits, and when she moves, single strands of hair jump up and dance around her head. Her voice is firm and her eyes bright.

One day, in that hot, airless room, she asked us what the predominant emotion in rape victims is. It was about half way through the year. We'd learned an immense amount, but were still shy of realising we knew nothing. So we guessed.

"Depression?"

"No."

"Loneliness?"

"No."

"Guilt"

"No."

And on and on ...

Finally, Professor Daniels rests her hands on her desk and says one word: "Shame."

For all my studying, for all my academic knowledge, I was just like any other rape victim. I felt dirty on the inside—stained in a way that can't be washed out. A voice in my head shouted over and over again, "No one will ever love you" until it was my truth. I was drenched in shame. It consumed me, and sat on my chest, not allowing me to breathe.

Why was I ashamed? Because of the way we were raised to think about rape. We whisper rape like it's a dirty word and think rape is when a strange man comes into your bedroom at night and grabs you. We think rape is always violent. We think that rapists are psychopaths, and that it's up to us to follow very specific steps to avoid getting raped.

These rape myths are so deeply embedded in our daily lives that it's only in recent years that they've been challenged, like in late 2014 when Columbia student Emma Sulkowicz carried a mattress around with her on the college campus to protest sexual assault. Emma says she was raped by a fellow student and the mattress symbolised how badly the school dealt with her complaint. Or the #EverydaySexism hashtag on social media where women give voice to their daily, lived experiences of sexism. It's only recently that we started challenging the patriarchy like this—for most of history, and for a large part of society still, rape myths are ingrained in the way of thinking.

For the nurse at the hospital, for the detective, and for many of the people who knew about my rape, rape myths allowed them to make sense of what happened to me. The logic is clear: I was raped because I was at a party, we were drinking, and my friend and I chose to go to the beach by ourselves.

The thing is though, when someone thinks this way, they're basically giving men permission to rape by refusing to hold them responsible for their sexually violent behaviour. And that's not okay.

I chose to do my thesis on rape, and I never once doubted that my subject was meaningful, important, and one hundred percent the right choice for me. What drew me to the subject of rape in the first place was the fact that it's surrounded by all of these lies that people believe about it. I wanted to argue with the myths, and I spent a whole year doing just that.

But I was a much better feminist before I was raped. Before I was raped, I could see lies for what they were—lies. After I was raped, I started to buy into these lies. I felt like I did something wrong. I knew it was my fault that I was raped. I am dirty, impure. Defiled. And knowing the theory changed fuck all.

The nurse is back, "You know what the world is like." Hours after I gave a lecture on victim blaming, the nurse was blaming me. And what did I do? I believed her. Maybe she was telling me the truth that my friends and family are too kind to tell me.

Mere hours after I tried to kick a rape-supporting culture in the balls, I was down on my face being kicked and kicked and kicked. *Stupid, stupid, stupid: what were you thinking Michelle? Thought you could win?*

And I can't get up. I can't stand. I don't believe in God—he never showed up. I don't believe the academic theories that I have spent hours and hours studying.

I believed the nurse. Because if it wasn't my fault, why the fuck did I feel so ashamed?

6.

ONCE MY TESOL COURSE IS FINISHED, I move back to Port Elizabeth to my mom's house. The idea is that I will stay there until I find a job in South Korea. I spend hot summer days lying on my bed in Port Elizabeth, watching the hours tick by.

My bedroom is upstairs, the hottest room in the house. The carpet is thick. I am spread out on my double bed. Sometimes I stuff my body with food until my stomach forms a rock-hard bump of pain and I have to throw it all up again. I watch my sweat drip slowly down my legs, the tears I cannot cry.

I don't feel much but sometimes I feel everything. I feel the softness of his tongue, I smell him, I feel myself still lying there on the rocks and wonder who this person is who came back. I see the world through a haze of anti-retrovirals and anti-depressants. They fog up my brain and cloud my eyes. Every time I try to do something more strenuous than a light walk, I vomit for hours.

Piccadilly's ears prick through the haze. My Jack Russell pavement special watches me and knows that something is wrong. She bites anyone who tries to touch me. Everyone looks at me differently now, except for Piccadilly. When I start awake at night, she is calm. Her eyes meet mine, and I know that even though nothing is okay, I am loved.

When I hear a strange noise and I get scared that someone is coming to get me again, I watch Piccadilly. If she doesn't bark, I know that I am safe. I wake up, my body shaking with sweat and fear, and her hot, little breath is constant against my leg. Her warm body with its soft fur presses against me, and I know this little dog chooses me above everyone and everything else.

It's Ashley's birthday. I wear a dress. It's the first time that I've gone out with friends since I was raped, and I know that we'll probably go to a club after dinner. Despite the heat, I put on stockings and a jacket. I cover as much of myself as I can and convince myself that no one will notice me. The restaurant is crowded, bathed in a warm, yellow light. The cacophony of sounds creates a shrug of comfort that I immediately wrap around my shoulders. I order a huge glass of wine.

Ashley, Ashley's brother and his girlfriend as well as my friend Rachel are already there.

"For you," I say as I hand Ashley her birthday present—a book and a purple vest.

"Awww, thank you my friend!" Ashley says and kisses me on the cheek.

As she talks to her brother and his girlfriend, Rachel turns to me. Ah, there they are: the "rape eyes."

"How are you?" she asks me.

"Fine, you know." How else can I answer this question? I want to be honest with my feelings but I never know when to say what, or how. I want everyone to know how horrible everything is, but I don't want to make myself a burden.

As we are talking a couple of other people come, including the guy Ashley is currently with. Ashley is the kind of person I ordinarily would love to hate: tall, skinny, blonde, beautiful, and smart. Unfortunately, we turned out to be best friends, and the option of hating her flew out the window.

I don't know any of the other people. Rachel, watching me closely (to see if I will crack?) sees my panicked expression, leads me over to them, and introduces me. There are five guys and two girls. I politely say hello and order another glass of red wine.

When we sit down, I start to talk to one of the guys. Brian, a guy Rachel introduced me to earlier, interrupts our conversation and asks me what I studied at university.

"Well, I have a degree in Politics, Philosophy, and Economics—"

"So you like to debate?"

"Yes, I love it. I have the power to win debates by the tantrums I throw alone," I joke. He's not amused. Granted, it wasn't a great joke but usually I at least get a smile.

"So, what did you want to become?"

"Well, I originally wanted to be the first female president of South Africa."

"That's never going to happen." He's leaning forward, an intense smile on his boyish face, a thin smile that curls at both edges. He's short with dirty blond hair and has an easy confidence about him. Someone who's used to getting what he wants, I think. He enjoys interrupting me.

"Why not?" I ask.

"Look, I'm just saying that given the current political climate in South Africa, there will not be a female president in, at least, the next ten years."

I think about it. "Realistically speaking, yes, I agree. There won't be but I don't think that that means there shouldn't be."

Despite his cockiness, I like that he doesn't treat me like I'm made of glass. Granted, he doesn't know that he should.

"So you're an idealist," he says like it's a dirty word.

"Yes, I am," I say.

He goes on a long tirade about how useless idealism is and how realism is much more, well, realistic.

"Being idealistic is not useless, it's about having an idea, beliefs, and goals that you are able to strive towards. It's not about achieving these goals. It's about having something that you believe in, strongly, despite being challenged. If we didn't have people who are willing to fight for unrealistic, unachievable acts of greatness, nothing good would ever get done and we would be stuck, never moving forward," I respond.

Before he can reply the food comes.

I'm relieved. I didn't know that I was still an idealist.

We're dancing. Ashley's on my one side, Rachel on my other. The alcohol smooths out the rough edges of my jumbled-up emotions into an elated abandonment. I dance, and finally, I don't care about anything.

We're at Beleza, the only place where we ever go out to dance in Port Elizabeth. Like most clubs, the dance floor is in the middle with the bar at its edges, all the better for men to mill around and pretend to talk while staring at the women. There's a small platform with a pole that gets used more than it should. The club is dark, but we're moving and the lights are flashing and there's alcohol. That's all that matters.

I think I like Brian. What I really like is that he likes me, in my jacket and my stockings in the hottest club in Port Elizabeth in the middle of summer. He sees me as someone who is desirable. He sees me as a woman. He sees me as sexy. That's what I so desperately want.

He doesn't see me as rape.

At one point I walk up to him and say: "I don't like you."

I am trying to pursue a man by telling him I don't like him. What I'm really trying to do is hold onto my power while being desperate for some kind of male approval.

"Then why are you still here?"

I drunkenly shake my head and dance away. This happens a few times until there's just the two of us. And he's very close to me.

"If you kiss me you lose," I whisper.

He kisses me anyway.

I wait for it to feel different or for me to react to the kiss. But it's not in any way significant or different to how kisses were before I was raped. A kiss is just a kiss is just a kiss. I breathe him in. It feels good to be wanted.

Maybe it should have been a bigger deal. But it wasn't. Maybe I should have waited for someone who actually knew and loved me. But I didn't.

So it wasn't someone who loved me. But it was someone who, in that moment, wanted me, and that was every kind of validation I was looking for. It made me feel like a different person, one who was sexually desired. Scrap that—it made me feel like a person. It allowed me to push the fact that I was sexually violated to the edges of my consciousness, where it took a break from drowning me.

At three a.m., six of us decide to stay over at a friend's house. On the way there, my mom keeps calling me. She's freaking out and wants me to come home. I'm so mad at her. Why can't she let me enjoy this little bit of fun? Why can't she let me have my first bit of freedom since I was raped? I understand that she wants me to be safe but I have this uncontrollable desire to let loose, to not care, to be normal.

She's ruining it, but I call a taxi to take me home.

Brian and I sit at the kitchen table and wait for the cab.

"I'm sorry," I say. I really am. I want to stay.

"No, it's fine, if you want to go, go," he shrugs and doesn't look at me.

"You don't understand, I don't want to go, I have to go!" The amount of alcohol I've consumed is causing my body to sway, completely scrambling up the logical part of my brain, and all I want is for this guy to understand.

"My mom is worried about me, I was mugged really badly a couple of weeks ago and…" I'm not going to tell him I was raped, I just want to justify why my mom is acting weird and why I, at the ripe old age of twenty-three, am going with it.

"You were raped," he says.

I look at him. I can't read his face. Even though I don't want to tell him what happened to me, I can't lie about this. It is in that second when I'm given the opportunity to deny it that I realise I never will deny it, no matter how much it hurts me and no matter how much I want to.

"Yes," I say.

He doesn't react. He doesn't move.

My delicate state of composure collapses, and tears stream down my face. "Please don't tell anyone," I say to him. "I'm so sorry," I say this over and over and over.

He takes my hand, "You don't have to be sorry."

I feel so bad for him at that moment. Here he is trying to have a good night and the girl he is casually hooking up with tells him that she was raped less than a month ago. I feel disgusted with myself for doing this.

I tell him I'm sorry, because I feel like I did something wrong. I tell him I'm sorry because I feel like everything that happened is my fault. I tell him I'm sorry because I want him to tell me what happened is bullshit and that I'm still desired.

"Mich, your taxi is here!" Rachel walks in.

Luckily, everyone is too drunk to notice the atmosphere between Brian and me. I leave without saying goodbye to him. Ashley and Rachel take the taxi home with me.

I lie in the backseat in Rachel's arms and cry. I cry while she holds me tight. I don't care about what the taxi driver might think of me. I sob and tell them what happened through my tears. I haven't cried like this since I was raped. The alcohol took the feeling away for a while but now it is allowing me to feel even more: it's removed every barrier in my way to feeling, and I finally access these emotions at their core. It breaks through the numbness and allows me to be hurt, really hurt. I lie broken in Rachel's arms as she tries to hold me together. My friends tell me everything will be okay. I cry because I now know I will never be what I was. I will never feel and have fun in the way that I used to. I cry because, for the first time, I realise how utterly raw and shattered I am. I cry because I know that no one will ever want to be with me. What guy will ever want me, the real me? The new me, the Michelle who is rape. And I cry because I am not alone. Because, despite everything, I have someone to hold me and tell me that they love me.

It finally feels safe to be less of what I was and more of who I am now.

The next day my mom and stepdad go to a medical conference in Switzerland for two weeks. I am alone. I roam the house, night and day, fighting with my thoughts. I sit down at my desk and try to put into words and numbers what they took from me. I scribble messy paragraphs that don't make sense.

I look for God. I lie in bed and pray: "I'm not okay. Where are you? Please come help me. I can't do this alone."

I open my Bible and read the verse that I have highlighted in yellow, underlined in black: "Come to me, all you who are weary and burdened, and I will give you rest." Matthew 11:28.

But I can't sleep. Instead I lie awake, and remember the cold rocks.

When you experience something like rape, your life-long assumptions of your place in the world and how safe you are are shattered. And when the shitty event is taking place, you try to understand it using the sense-making tools you've acquired in your life—in my case it was God. And when God doesn't answer, simply put, you're fucked.

I start to say things I never would have before in the hope that God will come and prove me wrong. I tell my friend Amanda, "If a man ever treated me the way God treats me, I would've broken up with him a long time ago."

She doesn't know what to say to me.

I invite my friend Kim over while my parents are gone, to fill the empty house. She brings a bottle of red wine, good for forgetting. We sit in the sunroom, listening to The Strokes. I feel the pressure lifting from my chest as we smoke and laugh and drink and the sun sets, casting a warm glow over the room that reaches into every corner. When we are properly inebriated, I tell her. And of course I'm crying. And then she starts crying. And Kim doesn't cry.

"I'm so sorry friend," I say. It's become my habit to apologise to people when I tell them I was raped.

"Mich, I love you so much," she says.

"I love you too."

"You know, you really are my inspiration, you are amazing and I admire you so much. You are like ..." She scrunches up her nose, "like ... you are a cockroach!"

"You know," Kim says, looking at me like I'm the dumb one, "cockroaches won't die, no matter what you do to them. They're the only things that survive nuclear bombs. And that's like you, you always keep going."

At that moment, I feel incredibly lucky that I have so much love in my life that when one of my best friends call me a cockroach, I know it's a good thing.

Kim's phone rings; it's her boyfriend Michael.

"Hey ... No, no it's fine. Let me just check with Mich." She puts down the phone. "Friend, I forgot that I told Michael and his friends they can come. Should I tell them to go somewhere else?"

"No, that's fine. The more people the better at this stage."

Kim's boyfriend brings his friend Paul. Paul stares at me whenever I talk. He laughs a little too hard at my jokes. We go out to a bar, and whenever I turn around he's there. I forget my wallet at home, so he buys me drinks. When I lose Kim, he finds her for me. Kim is drunk and obviously upset over what I had told her earlier, so we end up going home early. In the car he says, "I really, really like you."

"It's the eyes." Growing up chubby, you quickly realise that eyes have the distinct advantage of not being able to pick up weight.

"No … it's the way you talk."

"Oh … okay." I look out the car window.

Paul messages me the next day. And the day after that. He wants to come over to drink tea. I say okay.

"Hey," he gives me an awkward side hug with his right arm as he walks through the front door. He has a white box in his left hand. Before I can say anything, Piccadilly starts barking and tries to bite his jeans. I quickly pick her up and take her upstairs to my room. When I come back down, he's opened the box to reveal four cupcakes.

"Wow … thanks!"

He just smiles at me.

"So what have you been up to?" I ask him.

As he talks about coaching his water-polo team, I stare at the cupcakes. They are vanilla cupcakes with pink-and-blue frosting and tiny marshmallows. I slowly run my index finger over the frosting. After about an hour, he gets up to go to water-polo practice. When we say goodbye, his lips rub over mine. He gets into his white VW golf smiling like a kid who just got ice cream.

The next day we go to the Boardwalk and play games at the arcade. At first, I am too aware of my limbs, I don't know where to put them. Then, as I'm shooting planes, I start to forget myself a bit.

"Wow, that was really bad. Like, I'm a bit embarrassed for you," I say after I beat him.

He grins.

When we sip on cocktails afterwards, he talks about his friends and his sister, about surfing. I listen. After what happened with Brian, I'm censoring myself a bit. But, by not telling him about the rape, I feel like I'm lying. He casually places his arm around me and softly kisses me. After he drops me off that afternoon I'm sick. What is wrong with me, kissing boys left, right, and centre? How is it possible that I can kiss this guy and not feel anything? Shouldn't I be feeling something?

The next day he asks me to go to the beach but I'm too scared to get out of bed. The day after that, he wants to take me for ice cream, but I can't eat anything because the anti-retrovirals are messing up my stomach. When I go out to the club again he's there, so I kiss him. Then I ignore him the next day. He eventually stops messaging me.

But I keep the cupcakes. I look at them every day. They're beautiful.

My immediate reaction after I was raped was that no one was allowed to know, that only I could tell people. But now, I find myself constantly racing between denial and wanting to tell everyone I see that I was raped. I learned later that this contradiction is at the centre of the sense-making process for the victim.

Here is something no one tells you about being raped: it's not appropriate to talk about it to everyone. It's not okay to just blurt it out. Society creates careful boundaries around what is and is not acceptable, and talking about being raped to people who aren't your best friends or family is most definitely not acceptable.

When I see the parents of one of my best friends, a couple I've known for more than ten years, they act as though nothing happened. They give me a hug, like they always do, and that's it. This happens over and over again, until I'm convinced it must be some kind of conspiracy. Did everyone meet and decide that I wasn't raped and forget to tell me?

Sometimes I feel like running around screaming "rape!" over and over again, because I find it absurd that I'm not allowed to bring it up all the time.

When my sister passed away, everyone knew. We had a memorial service, and hundreds of people showed up. I received hugs and kisses from strangers. People I'd never met before would come up to my mom and me in shopping centres and offer their condolences. The school principal announced my sister's death during assembly at the start of the school year. They ran an article with a picture of her car in the newspaper. Her death and our mourning was public. But there is no acceptable ritual or public way to mourn being raped.

Experts say that for me to feel comfortable with people or my "community" again, they have to recognise what happened to me. And then do something about it. The community should punish the person who hurt me and make sure that I am looked after.

This doesn't happen. And we never hear from the police again.

Rape shocks and horrifies people, and interacting with the person who was raped is uncomfortable. There are no set cultural narratives that people can draw upon to interact with you. So, often, they ignore it. And then they move on. They don't get that you as a person, not just a part of you, is permanently changed, and no matter how much you want to, you can never be the same again.

7.

MY MOM AND STEPDAD ARE BACK from Switzerland. Almost every afternoon, my mom and I take the dogs for a walk on the field just outside our house. It's a cricket field surrounded by a barbed-wire fence. Just past it is the Boardwalk Casino and opposite is PE Technikon.

This particular day is hot so I'm wearing a short denim skirt. The late afternoon sun coats the just-watered field in yellows and oranges. Piccadilly relentlessly chases golf balls, which she then refuses to give back to us. I can feel the wet earth pressing up on my bare feet.

My mom tells me about their trip while she throws little stones for Nemo, our other Jack Russell, who stuffs them into his mouth. He has four in there. Three guys come up on the outside of the field's fence. I'm immediately hyper-aware; I know how vulnerable we are and imagine every possible bad outcome. They stumble, throw their arms around and shout at each other. They're drunk. I know if they decide to come for us there's nothing we can do. We don't have weapons. The dogs will attack them but maybe that won't be enough. We are too far away from the nearest house for anyone to hear us scream. We are helpless.

My mom isn't realising how freaked out I am. She's still talking. Then the one guy starts shouting and waving at us.

"Heeeeey," he is shouting. He makes more sounds but they are too slurred to make sense.

I freak out. I just know they're going to jump over that fence and come chasing after us. They're going to kill us, and there's nothing, nothing we can do about it.

My mom finally realises what is going on and how scared I am. She takes my hand, and we start to walk home. The further we walk, the louder he screams. I feel the breeze lift my short skirt and hate myself and my body. I hate that I'm a woman.

We pace away from them. He is leaning over the fence, shouting at us.

My heart is beating, my skin is wet with sweat, and I feel like curling up into a heap and crying but I know that if I do that he will kill us for sure.

We make it home that day.

The hyper-arousal thing is getting to me, but I don't know if there's anything I can do about it. It's a part of my life now. Just another thing that I give up: feeling safe.

The oscillation between feeling nothing and feeling like your life is in overwhelming danger can make your head spin. These two opposite emotions, and the extreme level on which they interact, is one of the defining characteristics of PTSD. You go on a wild ride between these emotions because you are trying to find the balance between them again. But you can't.

Human Immunodeficiency Virus. No one can tell me that I don't have it. They all say:

"You probably don't."

"Percentage wise, it is extremely unlikely."

But no one says:

"Michelle, you are not HIV positive."

Because they can't.

I take my first HIV test at the hospital right after the rape. Then it's six weeks of antiretroviral drugs and anticipation before I take it again. I start to understand why people don't want to know their HIV statuses. I always found the notion absurd—how can you live in the grey area not knowing whether or not you have a fatal condition?

But now, I don't want to know. I am perfectly happy putting the test out of my mind and living in ignorance. I don't care whether this virus is taking over my body or not. I mean, I do care but I would rather not be aware of it. I would rather not know. Being on the anti-retrovirals isn't horrible. I take so many pills a day already—contraceptives to keep my skin clear and hormones in check, anti-depressants—that it's just one more pill to pop into my mouth. I feel completely numb as I swallow them day after day.

My mom finally takes me to get the second test. The doctor knows my mom, and they talk about anything and everything except rape and AIDS. Their words create an intricate and careful space around me.

I watch as she pricks my arm with the needle. She misses my vein and has to wiggle the syringe. Thick blood particles squirt out: one, two, three of them. Then it flows without resistance. She takes the vial with my blood.

While waiting for the results I can't eat. The little that I manage to force down rumbles angrily through my system before disposing of itself in a violent, diluted blast. I lie still, and nothing touches me. I watch the purple bruise on the soft pale skin on the inside of my elbow and wait. While I am waiting for the results of my test, my dad is here, visiting from Canada. It's the first time I've seen him in over two years.

As I enter the hotel with its ocean views, I spot my dad sitting in the corner of the hotel lounge before he sees me.

He's slouched into an armchair, wearing blue jeans and a checked shirt which strains over his belly. A pastor's son, and the first doctor in his family, he slouches just a bit too much, his long legs crossed over one another. A few wisps of his remaining hair blow in the wind as he tugs his ear. In his lap is a black 'man bag' just a bit bigger than a clutch, with a strap that can fit around his hand.

"Hey," I say as I walk over to him.

He looks up and his cheeks crease as he smiles.

There's a home video of the two of us taken when I was about four years old. In the lounge of our first house in Port Elizabeth, my dad lies on the thick carpet and I run over to kiss him. I hide behind the corduroy couch, then I storm out to smack my little lips against his. I do it again and again.

Now, I startle as he places his arms around me. He is taller than me, and somehow both smaller and bigger than I remember. He keeps me in a hug for a long time as I stare at the wall.

After my parents divorced when I was nine years old, I gradually saw less and less of my father. We lived with our mom and were supposed to spend every other weekend with him, but this didn't always happen. When my sisters and I stayed at his flat, Roneldi, a teenager, would scream and shout at him. I can't remember the words they said to each other, but I remember how wildly my heart beat and how sick I felt whenever it happened.

In the year that I turned fourteen, he moved to Canada. The first winter he spent there—my first summer of high school—my sisters and I went to visit him. He had to work some of the time we were there so the three of us often wandered around alone. I remember Janah, Roneldi, and I walking out of the mall in Edmonton and into the snow for the first time. It was our first time in a foreign country. We wrote our initials in the icy white snow, with pink fingers stiff from the cold, and took photos.

Less than a month after we got back from our trip, Roneldi passed away in a car crash. As the years pass, my memory of my father also fades. I can recall the occasions we've spent together since on one hand. I forget what he smells like. When my friends talk about overprotective dads who don't want them to date, or the way they talk to their dads about their problems, I don't understand them.

Whenever I see my dad I can feel how much he loves me, but I don't know how to respond to it. It's only when I see his face that I remember how the sun has decorated it with freckles, the way years of smoking have stained his teeth.

My dad has always taken care of me whenever I needed his help; the best way he could do this was financially. He remarried a woman much younger than him, Ioanna. She's also a doctor who immigrated to Canada from Romania with her parents when she was a child. Last year she gave birth to my half-sister, Emma. My dad emailed photos of the baby right after the birth, and I spent hours looking at this strange pink bundle that shares my blood.

We both order salads and Coke Lights, and I tell him the story. I struggle to talk because the whole time I am thinking about the fact that I will be getting my HIV test results back that afternoon. I tell him about the rape, and he tells me about my sister whom I've never met.

My phone rings.

"Mom?"

"Michelle, I just spoke to the doctor. Good news! You don't have HIV!" Like it's supposed to be a celebration.

Despite knowing it's a big deal, I don't feel anything at all. My dad and I finish lunch.

I think I was born a feminist. During high school, whenever our Afrikaans class got boring, our teacher would say something like "girls shouldn't wear short skirts" just to provoke me into a feminist tirade and pass forty minutes of class. I can't remember a time that I haven't been righteous and indignant about female rights. I chose to do my honours thesis about rape because I, with all the idealism and arrogance of an academic youth, wanted to help change the world.

Being a feminist is not sexy. In fact, sometimes I think being a feminist is kind of like being the anti-Christ of sex. For some reason, there is this taboo about being a feminist and sexy at the same time. When you tell people you are a feminist, they get this glazed look in their eyes like, "Didn't we cover that thing last century? Please care less about equality, have a beer now and laugh at my rape joke." And, as much as I wanted to be the cool, carefree girl who fluffs my hair and talks about other sluts, I just couldn't. Too much was happening in the world.

After I was raped, I didn't have much feminist fight left in me. My thesis revolted me. I hated the idealistic view of the world it portrayed. Who did I think I was? I hated that person. I had spent a year researching rape to the extent that it was ingrained in my pores, but all that academic wisdom did nothing to help me, Michelle, the rape victim. Ashamed, I avoided it. I buried it and ignored its existence. I forgot all the hypotheses and statistics and quotes I had spent hours and hours learning. I turned my mind to different things.

Almost by accident, I read a memoir called *With the Kisses of His Mouth: A Sexual Odyssey*, by Monique Roffey. I devoured it; it was so completely removed from the sickness and physical oppression associated with the repercussions of violent sex that I was currently experiencing and had studied for so long. I wanted to read about how someone found pleasure in something that had only brought me pain. I read the book in one day. It's about a woman who pushes herself to the brink of sexual boundaries and comes back happier. I found it, not inspiring exactly, but liberating. It was what I needed to read to remind myself that sex is not evil. Sex did not do this to me, and sex can be enjoyed.

It took this book to make me think about how I experienced what happened to me. I didn't experience what happened to me as purely sexual. I experienced rape as the ultimate power play. I feel like being raped had more to do with me being female than it had to do with sex. The rape was an expression of power and physical dominance over what gender represents in our culture. The rapists got off on the fact that they had the power to reduce a woman—*me*—to nothing. The act of violating someone was more important to them than sex.

I also think the most sadistic way someone can express com- plete power over someone else is by taking what is meant for pleasure and recreation and beauty and turning it into pain and evil. Lloyd Vogelman, who wrote a book called *The Sexual Face of Violence,* published in 1990, pointed out that in most rape cases, the rapist's need to express his power and superiority over the survivor is the most important factor at play. Vogelman interviewed South African rapists, who said the following about rape:

"I was kind of excited, not sexually."

"I feel strong.... It feels good to make a girl scared.... It feels good because she is listening to you."

"I felt ... I was the best, I had put her down.... It made me feel even better ... to know I am a man because a woman is bowing down to you."

We talk about rape in terms of sex in order to make sense of it. We say, "the man was overwhelmed by sexual desire when he saw the woman in a short skirt." But none of these rapists mentioned sex, they talked about power. Very often the contempt they feel for women is also revealed.

Vogelman interviewed convicted rapists in South Africa and found that a lot of rapists admit that they don't even find rape sexually pleasurable, which is probably why they are able to rape two-year-old children and eighty-year-old women.

So, just like rapists not only rape because of sex, I didn't feel like my rape was only about sex for me either. I guess the rapist and the rape victim have that in common. It was about losing all sense of power and control and authority over my own body, which was what they intended. The loss of physical agency, the physical intrusion and powerlessness that came with being raped was what stayed with me and haunted me.

Before I was raped, some of my friends and I used to say that we would rather be murdered than raped. As a South African woman, I feel it's a thought that has crossed many of our minds. It's a lie though.

You grow up with horror stories about rape and the monster-man rapist. I have been scared of getting raped for as long as I can remember. The fear of being raped controls your behaviour—where you will go, what you can do, what you will wear. When it comes right down to it, I would rather let them rape me a hundred times than let them take my life. The survival instinct is stronger than I ever imagined it to be.

Here's a confession: I don't hate my rapist. I don't feel anything at all when I think about him. To feel something means that I would have to think about him and acknowledge he is real. And I can't do that yet. I wasn't sexually active before I was raped so I had no idea how that was going to be affected. I already knew that I didn't have much trouble kissing guys but I honestly didn't know how the rest of it was going to unfold. Even though the feminist inside of me screamed against it, I felt defiled. I felt dirty, unclean, and unwanted.

The feeling that I was basically a human shit stain couldn't be absolved by a statement like, "But you're not." It also didn't help when people avoided the subject of rape no matter what. I felt like I was walking with the phrase "I was raped" on my forehead yet there were people who would politely ask me how I was doing and what my plans for the next year were.

Every time people refuse to acknowledge that you were raped, or that you were changed by the rape, every time people ignore your hurt and won't mourn with you, every time someone blames you or looks at you like it was your fault, it feels like society is conspiring with the rapist. Because you, the rape victim, are the one who has to deal with its tremendous consequences completely alone.

My mom has a very specific tone of voice that indicates "DANGER." This tone of voice causes grown men to break down and cry in less than ten seconds, small children to suddenly lose interest in playing for the rest of their lives, dogs' tails to permanently get stuck between their legs and milk to go sour. While growing up, this voice, somewhere between fingernails scraping against a chalkboard and the cries of children being told there is no Father Christmas, permeates all my worst memories. Such as, "Michelle, we are getting divorced" or, "Michelle, we are bankrupt" or "Michelle, you are eleven and it's time to stop talking to the fairies in public." Usually, however, with two older sisters, the fighting would get sorted out before it was my turn to speak. Which meant that I was left unscathed by The Voice for a long time.

When everyone else was out of the house and only my mom and I were left, it took me years before I was able to even speak during a fight. I used to just sit and watch her while she would scream at me. She has amazing stamina and can shout about the simplest thing for hours.

After a while I was able to talk, negotiate, listen, and compromise during an argument. But I have probably raised my voice three times in my entire life. It's just not something I ever saw a point in doing before the rape.

One extremely sunny morning, my mom storms into my room as I am lying motionless on the bed, Piccadilly pressed against me. She uses The Voice. "Michelle, I think it is disgusting how many clothes you have. Have you even looked in your closet?"

She stalks to my closet, yanks it open, and starts to tear item after item of clothing onto the floor. She has small, stubbly hands and they won't stop grabbing my clothes and pulling them onto the floor. "The clothes don't even fit in there!"

She goes on. And on. And on. I am gluttonous. I am ungrateful. I am spoiled. I sit up on the bed and look at my red toes and the ingrown hairs on my legs. Her small chest is heaving underneath her black T-shirt. I look at the violent emotions crossing her face.

"Just listen—" I try.

"No, you do not appreciate what you have! Do you think everyone lives like this? It's disgusting!"

I struggle to breathe. My muscles tense. My blood boils in my body and spills into my head. Everything inside me feels like shooting out and killing something.

She's attacking me.

"Shut up, shut up, shut up!" I scream. I jump up and run across the carpet to push her chest—hard. My mom stumbles backwards. Her body slams into the white cupboards.

I shake. I have no idea how that just happened. My mom's eyes are wide and scared. I run out of the room and down the stairs and out of the front door.

The feeling of power is overwhelming. It is something I have never experienced before, having control over someone else, the power to shock them and hurt them. I have no idea whether it's good or bad but for that second it feels good. It feels good to stand up for myself and fight back. It feels good not to let someone else get the better of me.

I get into my grey Yaris and drive. Even though I'm crying, I feel powerful. I fought back. I drive and drive—to the beach, past the mall—but the driving is uneventful. There's only so many places you can go when you didn't get dressed and you have red, puffy eyes and no cellphone or money on you. But I have proved my agency. I acted and removed myself from the situation.

I would have to work on the execution though.

I go back to my mom who is sitting on the carpet in my sister's room, her back resting against the double bed with the wooden frame. I catch her in a rare moment of stillness, and I sit down next to her.

"I'm proud of you." Her brown eyes are filled with an endless well of love. It's the kind of love that sustains you, that you can feed off and grow from. It's a love that sees you as pure, no matter how you feel about yourself. A love that sees who you would really like to be.

"What?"

"For fighting back. All those years, I thought there was something wrong with you."

I smile, and she hugs me. Piccadilly jumps up and licks us, not able to handle that she's left out.

I can fight back now.

I realise that I can't distinguish between physical and emotional threats anymore. I perceive any emotional attack, no matter how small or insignificant, as though it is being made on my life. The problem is, I defend myself as such. I also realise that, after all I experienced, I will never sit back passively while someone attacks me ever again. I now know with a certainty that scares me that the next person who attacks me will have to kill me before I lie down and let them do that to me again.

Later that day, my mom and I go Christmas shopping. I am apologetically addicted to Christmas. I look forward to it all year long, and the kind of celebration I like is one that takes a lot of planning, time, and effort.

My mom and I decide on a theme of white, silver, purple, and blue to decorate our tree this year. I want us to buy a proper Christmas tree this year but they are too expensive. I feel sadder about that than I should at my age.

When my mom sees my face she turns her car around and drives over the curb to where they keep the real, living pine trees. Sparse, dry, and light green but sturdy and strong.

"Which one do you want?" My mom looks at me.

"That one," I point to the biggest one in the lot. Obviously.

An Afrikaans Oomie in blue shorts, and his son, help us lift the tree and take it to the car, but the tree's so big that we have to drive home to get the Land Cruiser because it doesn't fit into my mom's yellow Yaris.

Once my mom and I get home—to the furious barking of our dogs—we struggle to get it out of the car. Then we give up and drink wine while we wait for my stepdad to do it.

Once my stepdad gets home, we realise it doesn't fit through the front door either—he has to trim it down. The top of the tree is bent against the roof the whole of Christmas.

It is magnificent. Sturdy, strong. Alive. Shedding green. I love that green tree.

Christmas is less than spectacular, less than eventful. But I am surrounded by love. At Christmas Eve dinner, I have to say something special about my mom.

"My mom was blessed with a fighting spirit." Anyone who has ever met my mother knows that she fights, sometimes to the detriment of herself and everyone around her. I add, "So, Mom, thanks for fighting for me even when I can't fight for myself."

8.

I AM SENDING MY CV EVERYWHERE and spend my days furiously typing away in coffee shops. It's the middle of February and I am living in Cape Town again. After spending three months in Port Elizabeth, doing nothing, I realised that I needed to get back to some kind of life. I haven't heard back from the South Korean recruiters.

I am living in an apartment with Jessica, Ashley, and Mackenzie. We've been friends since high school. Now, Ashley is in her last year studying medicine at UCT, it's Jessica's first year working in marketing, and Mackenzie works as a graphic designer. My mom let me move back to Cape Town on one condition—I have to find a job. I am planning on working in a bookshop or someplace to pass the time before I go to South Korea to teach English. We live just off Kloof Street with a breathtaking view of Table Mountain. The flat has a living room and small dining area, a kitchen and three bedrooms upstairs. Downstairs, there is a study which we convert into my bedroom.

Although the room has a sliding door which leads to a small garden outside, it is tiny and dark. I have to switch on my light even on the sunniest of days. My mom buys me a purple sleeper-couch which I use as a bed, but it's uncomfortable and hurts my back. The room doesn't have cupboards so I have to hang my clothes on a rail. It is opposite the kitchen and I can hear every single sound anyone makes. I know whether it is Ashley making tea or Jessica making toast or Mackenzie opening a bottle of wine. I can hear their joyful conversations as I try to disappear into the sleeper-couch.

In Port Elizabeth, the days passed me by as I stared out the window, glaring at the sun. In Cape Town, every moment is a challenge. Hipsters surround me with their fashionable carelessness, big words, and even bigger ideas. They hang around in coffee shops and are always on their way to some new project or friend, while I try to look busy and feel slightly left behind.

I feel stimulated, driven to live more actively. I lap up the air, mountain, sea, and inspiration. Every weekend brings something new: a market, an art movie, a show, a restaurant, a club, a drink, a beer, a band. Just walking on the winding road of the Promenade with the waves crashing, feeling the frothing sea foam spray against my skin makes me feel alive.

I'm scared to leave my mom. I'm worried that I might be too emotional for my friends. I worry about becoming even more depressed in Cape Town. But I need to be out there in the world, doing things for myself again, even if they are as simple as doing my own shopping, cooking, and laundry.

I don't feel like my flatmates are just friends. I feel safe with them, and I am allowed to fully live through my emotions. In the afternoons, I'll be lying on my bed, ready to shut out the world, and Ashley will come jump on me shouting, "Get up!" and I know we have to go for a walk. I have no choice in the matter. It's what real friends do—they shove you back into the sun when all you want to do is lie alone in the darkness.

Without ever consciously deciding to do it, I spend most of my time writing about being raped. Writing is such an essential part of my sense-making process that I cannot *not* write about being raped. By putting my words on paper, I feel I can breathe again. I punish the page in a way I cannot punish my rapist. I feel too much and the page curdles with the burden of my emotions. Historian Joanna Bourke says, "By demystifying rape we make rape less frightening and more amenable to change."

I don't know if that's what I'm doing, but it is what I want to do. In South Africa we know a lot about rape. We hear a lot of statistics. We hear a lot of horror stories: a friend of a friend, a girl in town, a neighbour. We read articles in the newspaper that make us angry and sad about the state of our country, and then we go on, because we have to. We can't stop and be personally affected by every single rape story we hear—we would never get out of bed.

The thing about rape, however, is that it *is* happening to you and me. We like to pretend that rape happens "out there" in a "blank unknown space," but it doesn't. If I could count the number of times my best friends told me that "rape doesn't happen to girls like us," I wouldn't feel the need to demystify rape in the first place.

What is your definition of rape?

Is it narrow: rape is only rape if a stranger physically threatens you into sexually exploitative acts?

Or is it broader: is rape any unwanted sexual act?

While many people, especially women, agree with the broader definition, they find it hard to apply it to their own lives. By now, we all know that most rapes are committed by an acquaintance, but few of us act like this is a reality.

The first, narrow definition of rape doesn't require anything of us. It allows us to go about our days comfortably undisturbed because rape is something that happens out there somewhere. It is perpetrated by psychopaths only. It is always marked by physical violence.

The broader definition calls upon us all to become a little uncomfortable. To engage with the complex nuances that make up rape means we all have to take an unpleasant look at our lives. It's difficult, messy, and so much easier to ignore.

One researcher, Diana Russell, believes that the remarkable thing about rape is not that it occurs but that we have managed to see it as a rare and deviant act when it is so embedded in our culture.

Rape is not rare or deviant. It is all around us.

In my first year at university, I meet a guy through one of my friends in Stellenbosch. I'm studying Politics, Philosophy, and Economics and live in a women's residence on campus. My friends there are conservative, but fun, girls who also live in my res.

André is a nice, respectable, rich Afrikaans guy. The first night we dance in a bar to sokkie music. I'm blown away by him. He wears chino pants, a blue golf shirt and a white sweater. André has a narrow face with straight blond hair, thick lips. When he asks me to dance, I'm shocked.

Then he tells me I'm beautiful. It's the first time any man of my age had told me that. We kiss.

He says I can trust him. And why wouldn't I?

A couple of months later, my friends and I are at a Stellenbosch night club. Katy Perry's "I Kissed a Girl" blares over the speakers as young students drink, smoke, and dance in their stylish clothes. I haven't heard from André since the night we kissed a couple of weeks ago. I thought this was not because he didn't want to see me, but because of some other extenuating circumstance. So, after the third shot of tequila, I decide it's a good idea to message him. I don't tell my friends what I'm doing. I simply stand on the deck outside and type: "We're at Tapas. Plz come."

He replies: "I'll pick you up."

A huge smile lights up my face. Throughout my high school career and so far during my first year of varsity at the University of Stellenbosch, I've always been the single one. The third wheel. The sad girl. I've never been asked to a dance or out on a date.

When I read his reply, it finally feels like I belong. I'm excited for him to take me to his residence, Simonsberg; I've never been there before. It's considered very prestigious in my friend group if you get invited to hang out or sleep over at a guy's res. I was the only one of my friends who hadn't been. But instead of taking me to his res, he drives outside Stellenbosch to where his parents own a house.

I think, strange! But okay. Maybe he wants to spend time alone with me.

I'm standing outside. It's a cold night and I'm shivering on the damp grass in my blue skinny jeans and white halter neck top. He forgot the keys for the house and has to jump in through a window. I laugh. The huge white house is on some kind of estate and far away from anything else.

When we enter the house, I make my way to the kitchen. He's probably going to make me a cup of tea. I lean down and peel off the black heels I can't walk in.

He takes my hand and leads me away from the kitchen into the bedroom. It looks like a hotel room. Thick cream carpets, red curtains. The sheets on the bed are crisp and white.

He sits down on the bed and pulls me down next to him. He leans over. I'm getting a boyfriend so I might as well let him kiss me. Isn't that part of the deal?

As he undresses me with his cold hands, I think: *I'm not sure I want this. What harm is there? It's not like anything is going to happen. It won't matter once he's your boyfriend. Your friends have gone this far, nothing bad has ever happened to them. Should I be doing this? Don't be a prude, you're fine.*

I'm in the bed, naked. He turns off the lights, and I realise I need to vocalise my boundaries. Like I was taught. "I'm a virgin, I don't want to have sex with you."

"Okay, sure. I understand." He leans down and sticks his tongue in my mouth again, his naked flesh softly rubbing against mine.

I relax.

Then I feel him poking himself against me. Trying to get inside of me. What is happening? Is he teasing me? Is he playing around? What is that thing anyways? He pushes in.

I jerk. "NO!"

He turns on the lights.

"What's wrong?"

"I'm a virgin! I don't want to sleep with you!"

There's blood everywhere. On the sheets, on my thighs, on his legs.

He sees it, and his mouth twists. Disdain? Horror? Shock?

"You have AIDS!" He yells and runs to the bathroom. He locks himself in the shower. He turns the tap and tries to rub the blood off.

I stand outside the door. Naked, my thighs covered in my broken hymen, I try to teach him what happens when you have sex with a girl for the first time.

"When a girl loses her virginity, her hymen breaks. That's why I'm bleeding."

"But…"

"What happens when you push something big into something too small?"

74

"Who else have you slept with?"

"No one ... have you never heard of what happens when a girl loses her virginity?"

"Have you ever been for STD tests? Fuck, I think this is AIDS. This looks like AIDS."

"But I told you I was a virgin."

"All girls say that!" A pause. "How am I going to get the blood out of the sheets before my parents get home tomorrow?"

After a couple of hours he drops me off outside my residence. He asks me not to call the cops. We don't kiss as I get out. When I wake up my panties are drenched in blood. My vagina is tender, and when I move it scratches inside of me. I have to wear a pad to class.

After lunch, I tell my friends what happened. They think it's my fault. They don't say it, but they don't say that he did anything wrong either. Obviously. I went willingly, I was drunk. I only said no after I was naked. What a complete idiot I was to expect him to respect my boundaries. No one ever mentions the word "rape." I also thought it was my fault. For days, weeks, I wandered around campus, feeling completely drained and numb. I found myself wondering whether I was still a virgin or not. I had no idea. I found myself unable to trust anyone, not just men. Didn't he say I could trust him? Doesn't that mean that it was my fault?

A few weeks later we go to a party at Simonsberg, and we see him there. I turn to walk away as my friends go and say hi.

Rape has only been seen as a social problem since the 1970s. Before that, it happened at home but there wasn't much anyone could do about it. Rape's only been publicly recognised as something wrong for the last forty years.

Before that, it was something that women *let* happen. It was something that was simply a part of life. In a rape-supportive culture, when a women does certain things, she is consenting to sex. Therefore, if the man rapes her, he cannot be blamed. So, if a girl gets drunk, or wears provocative clothing, or goes to a guy's apartment, she consented to sex and cannot get raped. The thinking is that men will never be able to control their sexual urges and all women are the subjects of their desires.

I only realised four years later that what happened to me was rape. This incident had haunted me into doing my thesis on rape during my honours year; in the Psychology community they call research, "me-search." I know a lot of people wouldn't define what happened to me as rape. This guy, he's not a bad guy. He's not an evil rapist. He completed his degree. He is engaged. He will probably get married and have children. Maybe he'll have a daughter. And he'll love her and she'll love him and think that her dad's a hero.

He is not a pathological rapist, but he did hurt me. I know there are thousands, if not millions, of smart, educated South African women out there, denying exactly the same hurt to themselves, saying, "It wasn't *really* rape. Like, you know, not rape rape."

It wasn't rape because you know him, you still know him.

It wasn't rape because he didn't beat you up or hurt you physically.

It wasn't rape because you didn't struggle enough, you didn't actually scream or say the word "no."

It wasn't rape because he's your boyfriend or husband. It wasn't rape because you liked him.

It wasn't rape because he's not evil.

It wasn't rape because your friends, your family, your community didn't say it was.

It wasn't rape because you're scared of him and what he'll do to you.

It wasn't rape because it happened to you.

Guess what? If it was sexual, and you didn't want it to happen, it can be classified as rape. In these situations, you don't "cry rape." In these situations, recognising the hurt that a sexual experience left you with is a scary and brave thing to do.

Obviously, no one can make you say you were raped if you don't believe you were. That's for you to decide. But just to get real, rape is happening to you and me. A lot more than we would like to think.

In South Africa, people are tired of rape. We have "rape fatigue." We don't want to talk about it anymore. We don't want to hear about it anymore. We've reached and surpassed our point of saturation. In fact, we kind of just wish the whole problem will go away without us having to do anything about it. Like a really big pimple. South Africans have developed apathy about rape. Talking about rape is passé. There are so many new, more exciting social problems to concentrate on. Rape is no longer the "it" topic. So, for the time being, let's just move on with life. I know André has.

9.

I COME BACK TO CAPE TOWN with three bags, four boxes, and a whole lot of anger. It is seething inside of me, ready to boil over at the slightest provocation. I am angry, and I am finally ready to talk about it to anyone who will listen. In fact, I fight the urge to shout at everyone who walks past me on the street, to yell into their faces that I was raped. But not everybody in my life can understand it—or me.

Some people I know stop contacting me after they find out that I was raped. Others never talk to me about it at all. And I am mad about it. What is it about my rape that has inconvenienced you? That makes your life hard? All those thoughts about not wanting to "burden" people are gone.

I'm angry at everyone who ignores what happened to me. I am angry at the way the people at the hospital and police station treated me. I'm angry because I don't know what I'm supposed to do or feel. And I'm also angry because a couple of months after I was raped, people start to move on. The power of the mind and its adaptability allowed them to file me under, "the girl who was raped but now does other things." They have integrated it into part of who I am and what I stand for. It isn't on their radar 24/7. And why should it be? They have lives to live and things to do.

The girl who was raped is still stuck on, "Are you fucking kidding me?" and wants to shout it at people all the time.

Sometimes when you tell someone you were raped, they'll say, "I won't tell anyone!" While this would have been a relief to me in the first couple of weeks after I was raped, now it just pisses me off. Who was I protecting by keeping what happened to me a secret? I don't need to do that anymore, but sometimes I feel like it makes others more comfortable if I contain it.

One day I get home from writing at a coffee shop. As I throw my things down on the floor of my room, my eye catches my teddy bear, sitting on top of my bed. I am so mad that I decide to murder him. The world is no longer making any sense and I can't breathe and everyone is wrong and irritating and it's like everyone is trying to hurt me and my blood is trying to escape, it is gnawing at my arms, my feet, my face, just eating away at me so I take my teddy bear and I tear at him, I smack him against the wall. I throw him down and jump on him. I tear off his jean jacket and bite him. After a while I stop. I sink down onto my bed, curl up and lie there. I can't remember why I was mad.

Before I can go properly, stark raving mad, I hear that I have a job. A real job—well, internship—at a huge journalism corporation. I try to get it together; I can't afford to fuck this up. This is good. This is moving me forward. It's strange because journalism is a dream that I gave up in order to pursue Psychology after I realised in university that my depression and anxiety might make it difficult for me to handle the pressure, and here I was, stepping back into that world.

The people at my work are friendly. When I arrive on the first day, I am greeted with a big cappuccino and my own workspace. My own work computer! My own work desk with drawers! It even has keys! I get to keep the keys! Look, windows! There are people walking around, being all officious and doing jobs and typing on their keyboards to earn money! I hunch over my computer, hoping that no one will notice me, trying to blend in with the blue wall behind me.

Eventually, however, I realise that I have to go to the bathroom.

An hour later, I build up the courage to ask where it is.

"Past the lifts, down the stairs to your left," they tell me.

I nod. This sounds simple enough. Even someone like me with no sense of direction shouldn't be able to mess it up. I walk out of the office. The lifts are on my right, so I keep walking straight past them, into an empty office space. At the end of this office space is a big "EXIT" sign. This must be where the stairs are.

I push open the door. Stairs! I sigh a breath of relief as the door closes behind me. It is a dark, empty and slightly damp stairwell that is badly lit.

I walk down the stairs. For a while. After about three flights I realise that this might not be the bathrooms. I ponder this as I walk back up. How could I have misinterpreted the directions? Where did I go wrong?

I get to the door and push. It doesn't open. I push harder. Nothing.

Damn, damn, damn! Panic starts to swell in my throat. I didn't have my phone on me, and the office space behind the door was empty. I am going to die in the emergency exit passage on my first day of my first official job ever.

Think. Be clever.

"Ummm ... Help?" I squeak. "Help. Hello! Help!"

I realise that I'm going to have to make a lot of noise.

I bang on the door and make noises: "Hellooooooooo! Anyone out there! Hi! Hi there! There's someone on the other side! He—!"

The door opens. A very puzzled looking young fellow stands behind it and stares at me.

"Thanks!" I chirp.

He stares at me as I walk past him to the other side of the office. My toilet break has taken fifteen minutes but, luckily, no one comments as I slide back into my seat.

I still have to pee.

It is the most boring internship in the world. I spend my time sitting behind a big Mac, copying and pasting, checking facts, and taking screen shots. But I'm glad for the distraction from daily life and the structure. I get paid to do a job that doesn't require too much of me, and that suits me just fine.

I also start a blog.

Everything I am feeling, I put in the blog. After always being told to be less creative in my academic writing, I finally have a place to write just about me and what I want to communicate. One day my writing is political, the next I write some poetry, the next I post some images. My blog becomes the main constructive output of my life for the next six months, the place where I cut the insanity out of my mind and expunge it.

I end up working there for six months. Each month, my goal of going to South Korea and teaching English slips further away until, eventually, without me making a concrete decision about it, it vanishes completely.

One of my biggest problems at this stage of recovery is my state of hyper-arousal. The year before I was raped I was very active, exercising three to four times a week. Because I studied from home I went to the gym during times that suited me. Now, I have to go to gym during times that are extremely busy and I loathe it. I also hate being inside a gym building after being inside the office every day. After trying to go jogging or walking by myself once or twice, I realise I can't do it because I am too scared. Even during broad daylight a stretch of road without anyone else on it causes me to hyperventilate, to start looking around, always aware of danger. I end up nauseous and exhausted, sometimes crying.

When you have PTSD, hyper-arousal is with you every single day. Every time a homeless man walks behind me, I am aware of it, and I turn my body away from him, hand on my bag, even though I know this is offensive and wrong. Every single night that I park my car in the street and have to walk twenty metres to our apartment I am so scared I'm shaking. I get into the habit of checking under my car before I get in. I always carry my keys with the sharp edges sticking out and imagine, even practise, jabbing their edges into the throat and eyes of my assassin. I never leave anything to chance. I very rarely meet people at places if I know I have to walk in the dark by myself from a parking space. I also keep my phone on speed dial to the police or my mom.

I took a self-defence class in my third year of varsity. They taught us that a woman's centre of gravity is lower than a man's—it is in her hips and a man's is in his shoulders. They taught us that, when you are being attacked, you should target vulnerable areas like the throat, the eyes, and the groin. They showed us that by folding our palms into each other and bending our elbows into a triangle, we make the strongest shape that can be made with our body, and we should always use this for beating someone up. None of what they taught me was useful that night. I forgot all of it. Now, I am obsessed with learning about ways to defend myself, but nothing seems like the right way to go about it. I want to take another course, but why would it work this time if it didn't the first time? As for weapons, didn't my friend have pepper spray and a Taser? None of it will get rid of what haunts me the most: fear.

The worst is the lifts at work. We work on the twentieth floor where we have a great view of the Cape Town harbour on our left and Table Mountain on our right. It's beautiful. But there are a lot more men than women working in the building and every morning I get into the lift with a man or two men and look at the button they press, thinking, *"He cannot rape me in the time it takes to get to the sixth floor." "There's two of them, maybe they'll gang up on me." "Maybe he can do it in eleven floors, but he looks nice."*

I go through this every single morning for the six months that I work there.

My housemates are great company. We sip wine on our balcony during the evenings and talk about our days. We take turns making dinner for each other. On Sundays, we have our traditional meal of roast chicken and rye bread. We have TV programs we watch together. No one will sit next to me during *The Bachelorette* because I get too involved and start hitting them if things don't go my way. We look after each other. If I have a bad day when I feel I have to spend some alone time in my room, they leave me in my room. If they feel like I am brooding way too much they'll come disturb me and we'll go do something.

But I feel harder, like I can't sympathise with them. Like a part of me is gone, and as much as I try to reach her, I'm not sure I can. If they say, "I had such a long day," I would think, *listen, try getting to work in a state close to tears because the parking guard had decided to take out his handkerchief and I thought it was a gun.* They would say, "I'm so depressed" and I would think, *today at work, I was so angry after reading that a mentally retarded girl in Khayelitsha was gang raped and that the rapists made a video of the rape that was then circulating on the internet, that I threw up in the bathroom.* I resent their comparative ignorance and the ease with which they glide through their lives. I listen to their happiness through my bedroom door, the sounds of their unburdened laughter, as anger and depression punch through my heart. I don't want to burden them, but sometimes I hate how happy they are.

On Jessica's birthday we go to The Reserve for dinner with her parents and a couple of her friends. I'm speaking to a friend of mine about a few experiences she's had in life when she says something interesting to me:

"Then I realised, the things I've gone through in my life don't define me, just like your rape doesn't define you."

She is wrong. Being raped does define me. Being raped changed me to my core. But it's not the only thing that defines me. And I am angry that no one can see it and realise it. Why does everyone have to deny the fact that I was raped and that it affected every single part of me? That doesn't have to be a bad thing. I choose *how* rape defines me. *What* it does to me. I wonder when we became so scared of being defined by both the good and the bad.

I don't want meaning to come out of what happened to me. Because if it makes me a better, stronger person, then why would rape be a bad thing?

And rape should never make sense. It should never be meaningful. It shouldn't be something you can grow from. The price is too great.

But I do grow. I choose that it would not get the better of me, but it doesn't feel like a choice, it feels like the only way forward.

I am scared of a God that allows rape. I am horrified by the idea that God allowed me to be raped for the greater good, or His plan, or whatever. And the condescending smiles of those who tell me we can never understand God's will makes me want to punch them.

What I do know is that I am making the most of my life, despite what God "allowed" to happen to me.

I know a lot of people hate the term "rape victim." I absolutely, positively, loathe the term "rape survivor." Survival, to me, is a verb. It is something you choose to do. I did not survive being raped. I was raped. I am neither a victim nor a survivor. I feel like I have become rape.

I have always felt that a big part of being sexy, feeling womanly and wanted, is to be in complete control and awareness of your body, your sexual partner's desire, and your own sexual behaviour. It is extremely hard to regain your sexual self after you have been unwillingly stripped of your physical agency. What's even more conflicting is that the desire to be sexy, to have sex, doesn't go away. I don't stop being attracted to men, and I don't stop wanting a relationship.

I'm also stuck between two groups of friends. Some of my friends are virgins and will only have sex when they get married. My other friends have sex with their boyfriends or with guys they meet. They see sex as a healthy, natural, and physical part of life. I'm confused, and these two views spin round and round in my head until I feel as though I have a middle-ear infection.

And while most of my friends have clear transitions from virginity to being sexually active, and they decide when this movement takes place, I don't. I was raped. So, I know I'm technically not a virgin but I've never had consensual sexual intercourse. So, what does that make me? An emotional virgin?

At this stage my sexual history consists of André, my rapist, and a few drunken gropings. Not exactly an A+ performance. Not one to fail, I decide to tackle the task of masturbating. I go about it like a scientist—methodically, stopping every now and then to examine my thoughts and physical responses.

Nothing.

My friends buy me a vibrator. It's a purple, rabbit-like creature, and I stare at it in apprehension. Upon giving it to me they say, "we got you the smallest one because you're not that experienced sexually."

"How kind of you."

I try by just caressing my body. I lie in my bed at night and gently touch myself. It feels nice. Over time, I work up to using the vibrator, but not the big part because I'm scared it'll hurt me. Sometimes I try to watch porn, but after about five minutes it grosses me out. No matter how hard I try, I can't climax. I get turned on, but before I can enjoy myself too much a huge sign that says "damaged goods" flashes before my eyes. Still, I want sex and I want love. It's all I think about—wild, explosive, passionate sex.

But I don't know where to find this. So I look for it in everyone.

I down a glass of red wine to build my courage. I am going for drinks with a French boy. Matthieu. Which sounds like Matt with a sneeze at the end.

I arrive before he does at Van Hunks. It is awkward to sit and wait for him, like I'm already failing the date. I'm the one who is supposed to stride in, piccolo playing in the background, the wind ruffling my hair just so, while he sits and gazes adoringly at the vision who is me, right?

I order a beer and scratch at the label. There are two other couples in the bar. My bench is surrounded on both sides with empty spaces.

When he arrives, I am relieved that he is cute—I couldn't really remember. I'd met him during a drunken night at a bar on Long Street. He wears glasses and has blond stubble on his chin.

"Hi," I say.

"Bonjour," he says and hugs me.

The conversation is stilted. I do not understand the way he talks or the things he is talking about. It makes me feel dumb. I ask about things like the cigarettes he smokes.

"I like when girls speak Afrikaans, I find it verrry attractive," he tells me.

Am I supposed to speak Afrikaans now? I have no idea.

I slug my beer. It is warm outside but I am wearing a jacket.

For every sentence I say, he says, "What?" and then he speaks and I say, "What?" It's exhausting. I remember a story Natalie told me about the date she went on with a French guy and when she tried to leave early he said, "but I want to make pleasure with you."

I ask him what he does and he explains it thoroughly. I have to ask him five times, but I don't get anything except "office" and "exchange student."

"9gag, so funny, I look at ze site all day. Ze same picture for all the different things. A guy with a moustache every time. And everything 'like a sir.'" He laughs.

"My friend, she's always asking me about girls, and I say 'maybe, but not at the moment.'" He looks at me meaningfully. I don't understand the meaning.

After about a million false starts, I call it a night because I have to "work." Like copying and pasting is a very taxing job and they are very dependent on my unique flair for it.

And, he was all like, "Ze nice nite for a walk, no?"

Um, NO. Have you seen the homeless people that live in the streets of Cape Town? I have a hard enough time taking care of myself without going all kung-fu for a French libertarian who wants to "look at ze stars."

He walks me to my car. I am unsure about whether he will want to kiss me or not. At the curb where my car is, I lean in for a hug and his face moves towards mine. Kiss it is then. It is the kind of kiss that makes me want to wipe my mouth immediately afterwards.

This experience leaves me demoralised. If my life was starring Katherine Heigl I would be knee-deep in Channing Tatum right now. My insanity would be "cute," and my damaged past would be "an interesting character flaw" to overcome.

I push open the sliding door to our flat. Ashley also went on a date that night. She's sitting on the couch in the lounge, an after-date glow about her.

"He was so cute and we just talked and kissed and talked for like hours," she says.

I make supportive "awwww" noises.

Bitch.

"How was your night?" she asks me as I make my escape to my room.

I look at my face in the mirror. It looks so normal.

"Great," I say.

In order to break away from the monotony of office life I take a photography course with the camera that my mom and my stepdad gave me to "start my life." What I love about photography is that it's very different from writing. With writing I get lost inside my head, and sometimes there's not a lot going on in there or there's too much going on and it's not a good place to be. With photography, I get lost in the world outside of myself. Take the external and forget about the internal.

I am driving to Kalk Bay, which nestles past Muizenberg. Where I was raped. I don't know the road well, and my GPS takes me on the exact same path that we drove back from the hospital that morning. I remember seeing all the morning joggers and thinking about how normal their lives were. This time, as I drive in, I'm wondering who got raped there last night. I wonder who has just had their lives ruined.

It's cold in Kalk Bay. I'm wearing jeans and a green jacket. I approach the group of wanna-be photographers and our teacher. We are gathered in a parking lot right next to the beach.

"Good morning!" I say.

"Morning," everyone choruses back to me.

There's a girl.

She has black hair and a sharp nose, dark olive skin. I find myself wanting to share my space with her, wanting to be around her all the time.

"How are you?" I ask her.

"Fine, just not a morning person," she says.

"Me neither, I feel like being here at this time is similar to medieval torture," I say.

She laughs.

And then it's just me and my camera. But I am alone and safe in the best possible way—interacting creatively with my environment. I see a coke bottle lying embedded in the sand, a car tire in the distance. To get the perfect angle I lie down on my stomach, my hair flying in every direction, salt water dotting my red leather shoes, and fine sand making way for me.

I have to pee. I go to an abandoned public restroom where I'm sure someone will abduct me. No one will ever see me alive again. Luckily, after squatting over a toilet seat with cobwebs and drip-drying, I make it out.

I want to follow the girl but I don't, because she confuses me and I don't know what to do about it. I've wanted to kiss girls before; this is different. When I'm around her she makes me aware of every single part of my body. Would it be easier for me to have sex with a girl? I trust women more than men, but I've only been attracted to a few of them. The way her body softly curves around the camera is so different to the aggressive, hard movements of men.

I find myself thinking about her. Fantasising about her. She occupies me.

"Are you a lesbian?" Julia asks me when we go for drinks one night. I have been talking about Photography Girl and my desire for her non-stop.

"I don't even know if I'm bisexual," I answer. I'm on my second glass of red wine, and I sway to the beat of the heavy bass of whatever rock song is playing at The Shack. "I just know that I'm attracted to her."

"Interesting," Julia says as she clutches her handbag on her lap. It makes me feel like a science project.

"I've always been sexually aware of women, I just think getting raped ... opened it up? I don't know.... It's weird," I sigh.

"Do you think it's because you will feel safer, sexually, with a woman?" she asks.

"Maybe. But it's strange because I also have this overwhelming need for a man to protect me. Like, because a man did that to me, only a man can make it right ... if that makes any sense?" I grope for more wine.

My friends are supportive of my sudden sexual orientation confusion. Everyone wants me to define it. They ask how I would classify myself. I have no idea.

"Don't worry Ashley, I don't want to lick you," I feel the need to reassure her when we are in the bathroom one evening.

After one class, a group of us walk into a coffee shop. She is sitting there with a guy.

"Hi, this is James, my boyfriend," she says.

I am so much hotter than he is.

What a weird first thought to have when being introduced to a friend's boyfriend. Not that I wasn't hotter than him. I resent him. He has a large forehead and laughs too much.

When I leave, I know she's watching me as I walk away. I shake my head at myself.

10.

A FTER A PARTICULARLY UNEVENTFUL DAY at the office, I get home and I don't have anything to do. Glaring at me from my bedside table is *Trauma and Recovery*, the book that Dr. Adriaanse gave to me when I went to him right after I was raped.

It lies perfectly still, poised. Arrogant almost. I go to the bathroom, and I can feel it calling me. Giving up, I grab it and sink into my bed while I read. This is the first time I meet Judith properly, and that bitch knows every single thought and emotion I'm feeling. I like to think of myself as an extremely important individual, and here she is, describing exactly what I'm going through. Just in a much smarter way.

What's comforting is knowing that you fit into a category—in my case, the PTSD category. You know that you are not the first person to be going through this. You know that you can survive. You know that there are steps you can take. There are a few things that strike me as I read this book. One of them is that when you speak publicly about your knowledge about rape, you are inviting the stigma of rape to be attached to you.

By writing *this* book, I invite the stigma of rape. The stigma of rape is that I am dirty, defiled, that I asked for it, that it'll teach me to behave myself better, and maybe, if my vagina and I are lucky, some poor bastard will take us on in the future.

Well then, stigmatise away. My vagina and I can take it.

Something that really scares me is how vulnerable I am, and it scares me that no one else seems to realise it. Don't they know that we can all die? Without any reason, without it making sense, without waiting to see if we're ready, we can just ... die. How do we all not go insane knowing that?

One night, Ashley, Mackenzie, Jessica, and I are sitting on the balcony, sipping wine after work, as we often do. I have my back to the stairs that lead up from the garage. I am venting about my day. Jessica's facing me.

"I spent the whole day reading the farming magazine. Did you know there are more than five different types of cow breeds? I do. I even know their names—"

"Aaaaaaaaaaaarrrrrrrrrgggggggggggghhhhh!" Jessica screams. The scream chills my blood and shatters my bones. It is a scream that means death.

I jump out of my chair. There is someone behind me. He is going to attack me. He is going to kill me.

"What?" I ask. A quick look, there's nobody there.

She doesn't say anything. She's staring intently at the wall.

"WHAT?"

"There was a rat."

I breathe again.

"Wow, that was such a big rat," Mackenzie says.

I try to regain control over my body.

"Jessica, please don't scream like that." I feel shaken.

"I'm so sorry, friend. It was so big!" she says, laughing now.

I am mad. You don't scream like that unless your life is in danger. Life and death is real. Who cares about rats, they're just animals, they can't kill you or maim you or rape you.

"You shouldn't scream like that about rats."

"It was a really big rat."

But they don't understand. They don't know what it's like to look into the eyes of someone who has no problem with taking your life; to know that, without feeling anything, they can. And there's nothing you can do about it.

When I'm not mad or hyper-aroused or crying, I feel guilty. And according to Judith—you didn't think she wouldn't have something to say about this did you?—I feel guilty because I'm trying to turn what happened to me into a lesson so that I can take ownership of my life again. The guilt is supposed to make you wonder about whether or not you could have done something differently, which is a better option than realising you are helpless.

Well Judith, you're trying your best here, but that's not really why I feel guilty. I feel more guilty because of how I knew people respond to the rape than because of what I actually did or didn't do.

"Of course it wasn't your fault, you know that!" many people say to me, over and over again. Just saying this isn't enough to make me feel better. Harsh judgments or refusing to engage with my guilt just make it worse. What I really need is someone who engages with me. I don't want someone to say that I didn't do anything wrong, I need someone to talk me through it, to engage with it and interact with it. I need someone who will share the burden with me.

April 21 is always really hard for me because it's Roneldi's birthday. Roneldi was my eldest sister and she passed away in a car accident in January of the year I turned fifteen. She would have been twenty-nine years old; she was nineteen when she died. The worst thing with Roneldi's birthday is thinking about where she could have been now. If she would be married, where she would be living. If we would be getting along. Because for her last couple of years, we didn't.

When I was about seven and my parents were still married, we moved to a smallholding. It was their dream house that they had designed and built from the ground up. When we moved in my two sisters and I shared one huge room but eventually partitions were put up between the different sections. I was in the middle and I didn't like the walls going up. I liked having them on either side of me, always knowing what my sisters were doing. Every morning Roneldi's alarm would go off, and we knew we could sleep for ten minutes before Janah's went off and we had to get up. Now I had to wake myself up.

The first memories are good ones. My dad called the smallholding Ronjami (a combination of me and my sisters' first names). My parents bought a pony, Shatara, who Janah and I shared and a thoroughbred horse, Queen, for Roneldi. We had three dogs and two cats who regularly had babies. My best memories are of riding my horse and playing with my cats and dogs. Roneldi had a girl cat, and I had a boy cat. When the girl cat became pregnant we had their official marriage ceremony, signing their documents and everything. We raised the kittens together, acting as proud cat grandparents. Roneldi showed me how to hold and observe the little rats until they became recognisable kittens. She taught me how to feed the runts of the litter with milk through syringes. We spent hours lying in the grass, having kittens running over our bellies, licking our cheeks, hiding under our arms, curling to sleep in the crook of our necks. And when we sold them, we heaved great sobs of resentment and sadness, for we had named and loved each one of them.

I also packed picnic baskets for my imaginary fairy friends and then disappeared for hours to play with them. I would dream and play with the voices in my head. My mom once told me that, while she tried to encourage Janah and Roneldi to enter competitions and win things, she took one look at me and knew, "This child is not of this world."

My dad loved sailing and, although he already had a boat which we took out regularly, he decided to sell that one and start building a new one from scratch on our front lawn.

Every day after school Roneldi and I would ride our horses. My mom would make our lunch sandwiches and give them to us through the kitchen window as we groomed our horses, our tack lying on the green front lawn. I fed Shatara Marie biscuits and chocolate. We would gallop across the muddy hills of our smallholding, sometimes sneaking off our helmets. Roneldi, the fearless leader, on her Queen; Shatara and me struggling to keep up. I often landed in a heap on the ground. I was always bandaged, scratched, and bruised from some kind of accident. Riding scared me as much as it thrilled me.

Janah and I spent many afternoons in the lounge singing Celine Dion and Spice Girls songs to each other. We harmonised and took our performances very seriously. Roneldi and Janah did not get along.

My parents started fighting at home. My dad had lent my aunt and uncle money, and now we could no longer pay our bills.

A lot of things were going on but I was too young to comprehend them. I remember my dad sleeping on the couch. I remember my mom sleeping in the spare room. I remember finding bruises on my mom. I remember chairs crashing. One evening the fighting started while I was still in the bath. I was staring at the murky green water. It got cold. I was too scared to get out.

The door opened, and it was Roneldi. She grabbed a towel.

"Get out!" she told me. I jumped out, and she wrapped me in the towel. She took me to her room where Janah was also sitting. The three of us waited in silence until the fighting stopped.

Roneldi gave me my first book. We were both night owls and struggled to fall asleep. One night she took me into her room where she had a bookshelf filled with books by Joanna Campbell about horses. She gave me a book from the *Thoroughbred* series and told me I could borrow any of them whenever I wanted to. It took me a while to finish that first book but once I started, I couldn't stop. I started spending all my money and time on books.

When we moved away from the smallholding, Roneldi withdrew into herself. Our relationship was mostly based around animals, and we sold all the animals when my dad went bankrupt and my parents got divorced. We stopped talking. It's not really like we ever talked when we were busy with the animals, but we understood each other. We didn't understand each other anymore. She started flying off the handle at the slightest provocation. I was scared of her. She stayed in her room for hours on end. She weighed everything that she ate, including the tomatoes. She barely spoke to any of us. I discovered cigarette butts in the toilet.

When my mom remarried, Roneldi didn't want to have anything to do with Janah and me. She sat in her tiny, boiling room all day while the rest of us swam in the pool. On January 16, 2003, I was catching up with my two best friends after our holiday in Canada when we got a phone call at home.

Roneldi had been in a car accident. The hospital didn't give us information on how serious the crash had been, they only said to come as quickly as possible. I didn't want my two friends to come with me to the hospital but they came anyway. I didn't think it would be serious. I remember Roneldi being carted out of the emergency room in a rush of nurses, doctors, and my mother. She didn't see us. Roneldi was covered in blood and machines and wires and straps poking in and out of her little body.

I screamed. I couldn't let my friends touch me. They then took us into a pale room in the hospital where my mom came and my stepdad explained the basics of the accident. He cleared his throat a lot while he talked. Roneldi had rushed through a stop sign, not seeing the oncoming traffic. A bus had crashed into her. The driver of the bus later phoned my mother to tell her that Roneldi had been suicidal and had crossed the stop sign on purpose.

We were taken upstairs where we waited while they operated. Roneldi's boyfriend came. We found out that Roneldi had been driving home after breaking up with him. She had gotten in at Onderstepoort Veterinary Institute and did not want to have a long distance relationship. At this stage, I felt as though the whole thing was a TV show. I never thought that she would die. I do not remember how long we waited and how long the doctors operated and who came and who left. I avoided Janah. She knew me too well.

I was sitting with my stepdad on the uncomfortable couch in the waiting room when I asked him, just to make sure that she wouldn't: "Is there a chance that she could die?"

I knew he was going to say no.

He looked ahead, avoiding my eyes.

"Yes."

They were trying to get hold of my dad in Canada who wasn't answering his phone. My mom came and left a couple of times. Just as we were about to go home for the night, as there was nothing else we could do, the doctor came in. He sat us all down.

"Roneldi is brain dead," he said.

I could feel a part of me being ripped out. I fell to the floor, screaming, screaming, screaming and no one could touch me. My mom and sister sat quietly but everything inside of me was torn apart, and the hurt left my body in a gut-wrenching wail.

Then we had to say goodbye. My mom walked with me to where Roneldi was lying. She was clean. Somebody must have washed the blood off of her. Her tiny body was lying there, eyes closed. A pipe pushed open her mouth and pumped her lungs up and down.

"Roneldi was a gift," my mom said. "She was never meant to be." She looked at Roneldi like she was an angel. She was calm; a kind of certainty permeated her being. The nursing staff wanted us to stay and watch the doctor switch off the machine. They wanted me to watch my sister die.

"I can't, I can't," I gasped. The room was spinning. So many shades of green and blue. So many people and they're all fine. They stand and look, like life isn't leaving in front of their eyes.

Someone grabbed my arm, "You'll regret it if you don't."

"I don't want to!" I shouted and walked outside. I never had to see my sister stop breathing.

It's her birthday again. Someone who could have cared about me and helped me through this isn't here. I realise that I have two choices: I could either go out and get completely off-my-head inappropriately drunk or I could stay at home and work through my emotions. Like any mature, rational person, I choose alcohol.

Jessica and I go for drinks.

"How are you feeling, love?" she asks, her big blue eyes trying to penetrate my emotions.

I decide to meet Mackenzie. I walk to Slug and Lettuce by myself in the dark, Cape Town roads. I don't even let Jessica know that I'm leaving because I know she'll try to stop me. I know it is stupid. I am scared. I don't care.

Mackenzie meets me halfway. As we stride down Long Street, a street kid runs next to us and asks for money.

Mackenzie puts her arms around me. Never mind that he barely had the combined mental and physical capacity to beat up a paper bag. The boy runs in front of us. As he steps he shoves out his bum and makes farting noises with his mouth.

"I will fuck you up," Mackenzie says.

The Slug and Lettuce is packed to full capacity. We order flaming drinks. The rest of the night is a blur. Ashley joins us. We go to The Dubliner—it is loud and sweaty. I'm drinking, and Ashley, Mackenzie, and I are on the dance floor. The Dubliner is an old-school bar in Long Street. It is always packed with the strangest array of people and a lot of foreigners. Downstairs there is a band playing sing-along rock, and upstairs there is a DJ with more of a club vibe. So, the three of us are jumping around in front of the stage and I am jumping around so passionately that at one stage the guy playing the guitar points to me to come up. They're singing *She Hates Me*.

I take the mike and scream into it:

"She fucking hates me!"

Everyone stops. I don't think they were prepared for how bad I am.

"Lah, lah, lah, lah…" I falter, gripping the mike in one hand and beer in the other. Ashley and Mackenzie whoop loudly. Everyone else joins in, and we're back in action.

But I don't know the words. So I mumble along onstage and make some up.

"I try so hard but she looks like she's heading for a head-butt … lah, lah, lah, lah!"

The guitarist and the lead singer are laughing at me, and they end the song very quickly after this.

I wander around in The Dubliner and start talking to a black man.

"You know, a black man raped me," I tell him.

He hugs me.

"I am so sorry. But why bring race into it?" he asks.

I cry and walk away.

Ashley, Jessica, and I fly home to Port Elizabeth for the Easter weekend. At the airport, my blood sugar drops until I am pale, sweaty, and shaking. Ashley makes me drink a Coke. On the plane, Ashley and Jessica talk about going out but I don't join them, I don't think I'm up to it. I'm tired. While I'm standing at the baggage carousel, I see my mom and stepdad waiting for me. It's when I see my mom that I realise how much energy I have been using to keep it together. I grab my bag from the rotating grid and walk to my mom without saying goodbye to my friends. I throw my arms around my mom and she holds me.

I feel control leaving me, evaporating into thin air. All that is left is raw emotion. The dogs are waiting in the car. When she sees me, Piccadilly starts to cry and then she attacks me with love. She jumps on me and bites, licks, and scratches me with her little paws.

When I get home, my mom leads me to my room.

"I hid Easter eggs in your room!" she tells me, her hair bobbing up and down with excitement. "You have to find all thirteen of them before you can start eating."

We drink red wine while I search for them.

I spend the entire rest of Easter weekend in bed. It has been five months since I was raped. And still I have this bleeding shadow tied to my back. Everyone can see it, and I can see everyone looking at it. I can see their shocked and sad expressions, but they never mention it. The ones who stay, forget. They get so used to the shadow that they are surprised when I get tired of carrying it. They are surprised when the shadow carves into my flesh or when I don't have the strength to drag it with me every day. When I can no longer disguise it with pretty clothes and make-up. When it crawls onto my back and wraps its grotesque arms around my neck, when it pulls and pulls and pulls until I have no choice but to lie down with it, wrap myself in this bleeding shadow and find comfort in its emptiness.

That's what I do.

You might think that that long after I was raped I would start to be a bit over it. Apparently not. Because I sleep. And eat. I eat until my stomach is cramping and sore, finding consolation in physical pain that forces my stomach into a hard, unforgiving bulge of unhappiness. Food gives me comfort. I eat until I no longer taste anything. I eat not for the sake of eating but for the sake of forcing every one of my emotions into the pain of binging. Or not feeling. I eat to punish myself, to remind myself that I don't deserve to be beautiful and happy.

My bed suffocates me, forcing me to sleep and dream and dream and sleep almost against my will. I sweat and wake up with soaking sheets and clothes, freezing cold where the sweat had dried.

I lie completely still on that bed and know, without a doubt, that no matter what I do, no matter how far I run, the darkness will always find me.

And yet, being able to rip open the sores that had been forming is nurturing in a way, kind of like letting the pus drip out of an infection. Before this weekend, I couldn't deal with the pus. I was just ignoring it and letting it build until only a layer of strained skin was left. Seeing my mom is like poking it with a sharp, disinfected needle. The next three days, all I do is let it drain.

My mom lets me sleep and showers me with love. Oom Theunis is on call the whole weekend. I see him twice, at the airport and for dinner Thursday evening and again quickly on Saturday for an early dinner. At one stage the phone rings and as he hangs up, he says, "That man is as good as dead."

He gets his plate and starts dishing up a second helping of my mom's special pap en wors.

"Which man? The drunk driver?" My mother asks.

I feel sick.

"Yes."

"Is he black?"

"Yes."

And we move on to the next topic of conversation. *Why should it matter if he was black or not? Why are we, who have been so affected by death, discussing this man's life so casually?* It is almost like someone else saying, "I lost a file at work today." I couldn't help imagining that detective—the one who took the case and we never heard from again—telling his wife over dinner the next day:

"Two girls were raped last night," and dishing a second helping.

"Were they white?" she will ask.

"One was," he will say.

And then he'll take a big bite of steak.

He will never solve my case but, in his life, I guess that really doesn't matter all that much. And, seriously, when a woman is raped every three seconds, why should it?

I don't go to the church service that Sunday. Every Easter Sunday in the past we had attended the sunrise service at the beach. After the service, which is held, you guessed it, as the sun is rising, everyone would gather on the beach and watch people getting baptised in the Holy Spirit with braai smell in the air and the butter dripping down your hands as you bite into a crunchy hot cross bun. Crunchy because it's Port Elizabeth so the wind is most definitely blowing sand which ends up in your food.

That Easter I feel physically sick at the thought of attending a church service.

All those smiling, happy people. Singing and praising the Lord for "He is good." And then asking God to forgive their sins. Thanking Him for dying for them. All those pretend cheerful and happy people. Or worse, the ones that actually are happy.

I think I'm going to have to fight my mom about it but it turns out that she had lost God as well. I guess that's what happens when your one daughter dies and the other one gets raped. I needed someone to look after my mom after I was raped because I couldn't. I couldn't be there for her. But no one did. No one could see past the lonely, angry, scared woman, who had lost so much. No one could reach past her bravado to try and be there for her. She was completely alone, and it broke my heart.

She started telling people that she's an atheist, which led to her being ostracised in the community. She was angrier than I had ever seen anyone be, but her anger came from hurt. She still found it in herself to let strangers who didn't have homes stay with her.

So, there we are: my mom and I, the condemned. And I would rather be held by my mother with confusion and hurt than be hugged by a Christian with a fake smile.

If this is the life that I am living, I really don't understand what Jesus died for. Did He really die so that a man could rape me and then go to heaven? Meanwhile, I am left unable to piece myself together again, unable to acknowledge God or His love because I feel so betrayed. Do I then go to hell? But the man who raped me, if he accepts God's love and asks for forgiveness, he gets to go to heaven?

The only thing that has been great about God's love in my life has been its absence: a great gaping hole where God's love was supposed to be.

A few days before the Easter weekend, I had sushi with a friend at Sevruga, a restaurant at the Waterfront in Cape Town. As we gazed over the harbour and manoeuvred giant tempura prawns onto our chopsticks, she said, "After you were raped I was really angry at God, and I couldn't understand why He would allow that to happen to you."

"Join the club."

"I was struggling with it a lot. But then I read this piece in the Bible and I realised I'm not supposed to understand. God spoke to me and I worked through it."

I felt so betrayed. Beyond betrayed. I go around proclaiming I don't believe in God anymore and how dare He not prove me wrong? And how dare He help a friend deal with me being raped and not help me, the person who was raped?

I want to believe that God exists. I keep waiting for someone, something, to prove me wrong. But no, I do not want to hear about how much He does for you in your life when He can't even be bothered to throw a high five in my general direction.

11.

AFTER EASTER I LIVE INSIDE a thick, heavy fog. I can't see or hear or feel anything. Sometimes someone gets close enough for me to see them and for them to touch me. But then I lose them again and I'm alone.

Malini comes down from the small town in the Eastern Cape where she lives with her mom to interview for counselling jobs in Cape Town. I invite her and some friends who also did Psychology honours with us to the flat for dinner. I make my famous vegetarian pasta with whole wheat pasta, almonds, spinach, sundried tomatoes and feta, lots of feta.

We have dinner with my digs mates and then they leave, and the four of us chat about our respective "futures."

"I don't understand. They train us for a year, work us to death, and then, boom! No viable career options," I say.

"I know, they tell us how smart we are, how many skills we are accumulating but we are unemployable!" Malini says.

"It sucks because we actually want to help people. We are some of the few people out there who want to help people for a living, but after honours we don't have any way to do it really," Sarah adds. She is small, blonde, and flaps her pale hands in the air as she talks.

"You know, I studied for five years, and now I have a job copying and pasting. I get paid to copy and paste, and there's a girl in my office who's nineteen and she has exactly the same job and gets paid the same as me! I don't even have an ego left. How can they not see how amazing I am?" I say. I sink my head onto the table. A sundried tomato sticks to my forehead.

"They make me feel useless all the time at my job. They check up on every single thing that I do like I'm some kind of idiot." Naledi works at a marketing company. Her short bob accentuates her thick, tangled lashes and high cheek bones.

"Or we could study further, which costs more money, which will give us even fewer practical skills, which will make us even less employable!" I say.

"I'm just so tired of sitting at home. And I have all these 'options.' What am I supposed to do with these 'options?'" Malini asks.

"I have no idea. They're all like, you have your whole life ahead of you, take it easy, figure things out. I have no idea what I want to do with my whole life! And I can't expect my mom to always help me out," I respond.

"I know, I have to work for free at the moment." Sarah is interning at an addiction clinic.

"And nothing ever works out the way you think it will. Because you have this idea that you're going to be an amazing counsellor or journalist or whatever and it turns out you don't even like working," Malini says.

"That's why there's wine," I say.

"Wine will never leave you," Naledi proclaims. "Cheers to wine!" We clink our glasses together.

They are suffering from a severe case of the "now whats?" During schooling we were measured in yearly yardsticks of achievement and then, when we graduated, everyone was like: "Oh, and here's the rest of your life." While before I would have worried myself sick about this, now I couldn't really get myself to care. I used to run through life with a predatory anxiety snaking around my stomach, hissing at me to move, move, move, work, work, because time is ticking and the world is running and if I don't push, push I might never get to where I have to be.

It's gone. And there's nothing to replace it.

Later, Malini and I are sitting in my bedroom. It's just the two of us, and she sits on my swivel chair. I'm telling her about André—I had never told her about him before. Malini and I tend to share things with each other we don't always share with other people. I think we understand each other on a deeper level than most people.

Maybe it's just the wine, but Malini has tears in her eyes. "You know, you're the kind of amazing that can only come from being fucked up."

Which I think is a compliment.

"I swear a lot more now than I used to before I was raped," I tell her, while pulling off a loose nail.

"Why?"

"I think ... it's because I live my life through language. Words are everything to me. And rape is the biggest swear word there is, don't you think? And I've been forced to incorporate it into my everyday life. To use it over and over again. Rape, rape, rape, raperaperaperaperape. After a while, all other words kind of lose their meaning. Like what is a fuck, a shit, a cunt—when you compared it to rape?"

"You're right, it's nothing," she says.

Sometimes I think that the rape was some kind of new-age boomerang. You know, like *The Secret* by Rhonda Byrne? What you put into the world comes back to you? You visualise a parking space and you will get one. I tried that with an economics test in my first year. I failed the test.

Anyway, I was really into *The Secret*: I watched the movie, I read the book, and I even had my own "visualisation" scrapbook where I put all my dreams, wishes, and all that I hoped to accomplish. A flat Britney Spears stomach was high on the list.

And while what happened to me didn't follow this theory exactly, I spent the whole of 2011 on rape. I took rape and made it mine. Each day I delved deeper and deeper into all that it meant and contained—its consequences, why it happens, its rationalisations, when it happens. I studied feminist theories, developmental theories, psychopathology, cultural structures, and norms. I studied male sexuality. All of this knowledge was stitched into my skin, before I was raped.

I spoke to male students about rape. Extensively. I spoke to them about what they think about rape, how they perceive rape. I debated rape with them. The topic flowed from inside of me and over into these discussions as naturally as any other part of my history that I have ever had to talk about.

Even though the study was specifically for male students, girls came to me and asked to be interviewed. I was an inexperienced researcher and wanted all of the practice that I could get so I interviewed them. But that wasn't the only reason. Before I started each interview, I knew why they were asking to be there. They had been raped and they wanted to know what made me care about rape to the extent that I was doing research on it, and I knew how to speak to them.

My friend at the honours party recognised this, and came to me for the same reason. And in the bonding process of healing and love and counselling about rape, we were raped.

I'd focused my life so completely on rape, was the only possible outcome for me to be raped? I know it's silly to compare this to *The Secret*, but I can't help thinking that way. I can't help wondering if it was my fault.

My housemates and I decide to have a Digs Formal, with dates and a big dinner. We have a theme, Famous Couples, and I want to be Angelina Jolie and Billy Bob Thornton, because then I would get to wear leather and have tattoos drawn. Ashley and Mackenzie organise a date for me—Josh, one of Ashley's friends.

We spend the afternoon mixing two bottles of gin, a couple of bottles of wine, and orange juice into some kind of cocktail-like substance. Ashley and I cut up black bags and spread them across the carpet, taping them together and at the corners of the room. Spills avoided.

Mackenzie draws a dragon tattoo on my right arm while Ashley puts on her cowboy boots and hat and short shorts. Malini wears a mini-dress for her role as Bond girl and Jessica has a skin-tight batgirl costume she wriggles into.

We're ready. I'm nervous when Josh walks up the stairs, but his arms are covered in more tattoos than mine and we immediately start joking around.

I have fun chatting with Josh; he is easy-going and I don't have to make a weird sneezing noise in order to pronounce his name.

We have pizza on the carpet that we covered with black bags. At one stage I decide to put on a glittery, green hat.

"If Angelina had a hat like this I think she would wear it," I tell Josh.

"I agree," he nods solemnly.

I enjoy Josh because he knows how to treat me and I can tell he's a complete person. We go to Deco Dance, a club where everyone dances, has two sips of beer, and then goes back home. We're making out on the couch when I fall off it and start laughing. When we go to my bedroom, we get undressed. I do it almost without thinking.

I'm scared to tell him to stop because 1) I don't want him to think I'm a prude and 2) what if he doesn't listen and 3) how did we get here anyway?

"Can we just cuddle for a bit?"

He draws me to him and wraps his naked body around mine. I listen to him breathe. I wonder how I turned into the girl who can't draw boundaries. The girl who feels like she has no authority in bed.

I used to want to be virginal and pure. I missed out on that boat because I never defined myself sexually; I have no idea how to act or where to draw the line when I'm with a guy. I have never been respected and I have no idea how to respect myself. I want to be virginal and pure but I also want to be sexy and sexually empowered.

The next morning I wake up to the sounds of everyone laughing outside, so I join them.

When Josh tries to talk to me, I look away from him. He chats to the others, but I never make eye contact. When my housemates crawl into Ashley's bed to watch a movie together, I get in next to them. Josh looks at us and knows he's not welcome.

"Bye," he kisses my cheek.

I'm relieved when he's gone.

I have no idea how to speak to or interact with men anymore. I also have this vague feeling that they would dislike me severely if they ever got to know me, the real me. Add the rape to that … well. Overall, I thought it was better to pretend, to flirt, and to get drunk. As previously mentioned, being raped didn't take away my sexual desires. A lot of the time, I want to let loose, be carnal and go for it without worrying about all my baggage and all of my Feelings and Emotions. But I learn the hard way, you can't outrun your feelings, no matter how hard you try.

When Mackenzie gets home from work, I often join her outside on the porch for a smoke. This week, I'm still raw from my experience with Josh. What I appreciate about Mackenzie is that she doesn't press me with questions. I cannot handle being prodded like a herded chicken when I am trying to sort things out in my head. When I'm upset, I usually go to my room and think things over. About an hour later, I'll come out, ready to talk. Mackenzie and I sit on our porch, zip up our hoodies and smoke our cigarettes.

"So, how's work?" I ask.

"Same old," she replies. "How are you?"

I shrug.

We inhale our cigarettes. I stare out at Table Mountain. Clouds cascade over its edges, almost touching our heads.

"I feel like rape is all that I'm worth," I tell her blandly.

We exhale.

"Mich, don't you think that, maybe, you want to talk to other girls who have been through this? Because no matter how much we try, we're never going to get what you're going through."

I realise I want to speak to other people who have survived rape. It's useless for me to continue blaming the people who love me for not understanding me when they are doing their best to be there for me. I want to speak to other women who are strong and have survived being objectified and having their agency completely taken away from them. I have been in therapy for a long time, and that's not what I need; I know how to embark on a personal journey of exploration and sense-making and empowerment. What I want is a community of empowerment, healing and love. Where women could look at me and we could understand each other without having to speak and speak and speak.

Over the next week, I spend hours upon hours on the internet. I can't find a support group in the Cape Town area. I send out more than a couple of unanswered emails. Building up courage, I finally phone a clinic. I make the phone call in the middle of the street during my lunch hour. I work in an open plan office, and want to get the call over and done with. I walk to a quiet corner.

"Hello?"

"Hi, my name is Michelle Hattingh. I would just like to know—are you running any rape survivor support groups at the moment?" As soon as I say my name I feel like an idiot. Couldn't I be smart enough to at least pretend to be phoning for a friend?

"No, sorry, we are not. We have found, in the past, that too few people show up and it's too hard to keep track of people."

I keep quiet.

"Also, if you want to qualify for group counselling, you have to attend individual counselling sessions first."

The thought curdled my stomach. I've spent millions of hours in one-on-one therapy with psychologists, and it's the last thing I want to do. I don't want some tannie who did a counselling course to ask me how I am feeling. I want to talk to women who were raped about how it happened to them. I want to know whether they were able to make sense of it, and how they did it. I want a community.

"Can you refer me to any other rape survivor support groups?"

"No, sorry, I cannot."

I hang up the phone. People walk past me as I quickly punch the tears off of my face.

What was I supposed to do now, place an ad on Gumtree?

"Hey rape survivors, give me a shout? YOLO!"

Julia has this theory that you can find anything on Gumtree so I'm not completely convinced that this wouldn't have worked ...

I don't want to start my own group. I have such a need for someone to take care of me, and I don't have the emotional strength to create a healing and loving space for others. And I feel like a failure because I can't.

More women are raped in South Africa than anywhere else in the world—we all know this. So many women are raped in South Africa that everyone's developed an indifferent attitude, turning their eyes away from newspaper headlines, their thoughts away from reported stories, and their hearts away from victims. Sorry—survivors.

So that's how I end up as a survivor in the country with the highest rape stats in the world unable to find a support group.

Do they all just carry it in their hearts, alone? How on earth could we all be alone in this? In that moment, I feel my heart breaking for all the women like me, all the women who have been raped and sexually coerced or threatened. I feel broken for them. I felt their pain and suffering, and I hate that they had to go through it. I hate that they ever have to feel sad or guilty about this. I hate that they were born into bodies that other people felt the right to take ownership of. I hate that they ever had people judge or stigmatise them. I hate that they probably felt like they couldn't tell people and that they couldn't be loved. I hate that they try to justify it. I hate that, after everything they've been through, people make rape jokes and comments like, "We don't need feminism anymore," or, "Feminist chicks need to calm down."

I'm not crying for me anymore.

As I drive home one afternoon, I stop at a red light and look right into the face of a man trying to sell a newspaper. In that moment, I realise that this man could be my rapist and I wouldn't know. I stare into his eyes and wonder what my rapist is doing right now. If he is eating, sleeping, pissing, fucking. I wonder if he thinks about me like I think about him. I worry sometimes that I might walk past him on the street. I worry that I'll recognise him. I worry that I won't. I worry that he'll recognise me. I worry that he won't. Was he able to forget me?

I know that the police will never solve the case. We haven't had so much as a courtesy phone call to let us know how the case is going since the night I was raped. Our file is probably lying somewhere, forgotten, between a stack of newspapers and some real, important cases. Not cases of girls who got themselves raped.

But honestly, I don't want my case to be solved. I don't want my case to go to court. I don't see the point in putting myself through this, knowing what they'll say about me, how they'll paint me. Knowing I'll have to look at him day in and day out and that he might walk free.

My sister was involved in a rape trial. After I was raped, she told me I was much better off if it didn't go to trial. She told me that the opposition would take all my worst fears and thoughts and use them against me. And I believe her. I don't know if I have enough faith in the court to believe that they won't blame me.

I was taking a taxi home last year, while I was doing my thesis about rape. The guy asked me what I was studying and I told him. He asked me what my thesis was about and I told him. This was before I was raped.

"But you know, they always look at the man. But a lot of these girls, their behaviour, from what they are doing, these girls should also be blamed," he said. As I got out, I noticed his big hands on the steering wheel.

12.

ONE FRIDAY I'M ON MY WAY to meet Julia for a date at The Dog's Bollocks, my favourite burger place in Cape Town. It's located in an alley, and the owner only makes about fifty burgers every evening and they are as big as your face. I'm taking a shortcut from work because I'm already late.

I am waiting for the lights to change.

"*Beeeeeeeeeeep!*"

I jump. I was in front and hadn't seen the green arrow. I stomp the gas and yank my steering wheel to the right.

"Aaaaaargh!"

I underestimate how sharp the turn is. I bump over the curb. In the split second after my car hits the curb I think: *Please don't let it be bad, please don't let it be bad, please don't let it be bad.*

The entire weight of the car shifts to the right as we *clunk, clunk* along, steering wheel careening wildly about.

It's bad.

"Shit, fuckitty, shit-tittty, fuck, fuck, fuck!"

I park my car next to a robot.

Not only do I have no idea where I am as I was taking a new shortcut, I also don't have a spare tire. About two months previously, I got a flat at work and I had never gotten it fixed.

"You absolute fucking idiot Michelle!" I roar at myself.

The sun is starting to set over Table Mountain, the colours pink, magenta, and burnt orange. I am in no position to appreciate the beauty of it. I am stuck alone in a car, no spare tire.

And it is not the best part of town. I also have no way of defending myself. For the thousandth time I curse myself for not having been able to magically transform into a martial-arts heroine as I would have if I were Angelina Jolie. One of the many drawbacks of being Team Aniston?

I feel like I am about to break.

No. I can't. I take a breath, and phone my mom. Clearly, dryly, I tell her what happened. She responds in the same way. She knows we have to take action. She gives me the number of the AA. Since I don't have a spare tire, I have to phone them so that they can come tow me.

As I hang up, I want to break again.

Stop it, I tell myself sternly.

I phone the AA.

Ten minutes later, and they apparently have a unit that is "in the area" and will take anywhere from half an hour to an hour to come get me. I phone my mom and tell her. She is relieved and tells me that she loves me.

I take a deep breath and phone Mackenzie.

She doesn't answer.

Taxis pass me. They are bigger than my Yaris. They all watch me, as if they are sharks waiting for me.

I phone Jessica.

"Hello?"

"Jess, I'm stuck, I hit a curb and my tire is flat and I'm by myself and I don't know what to do!" I scream.

"Shit. Shit friend. What happened?"

I repeat it.

"Okay, okay."

"Where's Mackenzie?"

"She's here with her sister."

"Put her on."

I wait.

"What happened?"

I repeat it again.

"Okay. Okay. We're on our way. Where are you?"

I tell her the street name.

"Okay. We're on our way. We're coming now. Okay?"

"Okay. Please hurry, the men in the taxis scare me. I'm alone and I'm scared."

I message Julia to tell her what happened. She says she will try and find me as well.

It's getting darker. I touch my forehead and my hand comes away wet.

"Doef, Doef."

I look next to me. A taxi driver had gotten out of his taxi. With a wide smile he is banging on the window and trying to open my passenger door. If I hadn't locked it, he would be inside.

"Open!" he yells.

I shake my head no. He bangs his fist on the window. The light turns green, and he jumps back into his taxi and leaves.

The minutes tick by. I message Julia again. I phone Mackenzie. I speak to my mom. As long as I am on the phone, someone will know if something happens to me. I hear my heart beating. The sun disappears, uncaring. The police drive by. They look at me, make eye contact, and drive away.

I watch the last, pink limbs of sunlight disappear behind Table Mountain. Finally I let the tears fall. I hate myself for continually getting into these situations. This doesn't happen to anyone else, just to me. So, obviously, it has to be my fault. I will probably be raped again by the time anyone finds me.

I hate myself for attracting so much disaster. Like how I lost four wallets last year and the woman at the desk simply started silently handing me forms when I walked into the police station. Like how my car looks like a bumper car because I drive into a wall or lamp post every second week. Sometimes it's amusing, but at times like these I just hate the drama that comes with being me.

My phone rings.

"Hello?"

"Hi! I'm in the street, where are you?" It's Mackenzie.

"I'm at the robot." I get out to make myself more visible.

"Oh, there you are!" She hangs up.

She parks her little black Citroen across the street from me. She runs across the street as I hop up and down with joy: someone has come, someone cares! I am not alone in this world!

When she is close enough I jump into her arms. We hug for a long time while I cry and pull myself together. I am not alone.

"Here," she holds out a cigarette and a lighter for me.

I laugh as I light it. She knows me well. Mackenzie, her sister and I stand chatting. Julia's white Corsa rams up the sidewalk in front of us. Someone else loves me as well! I am loved! I run to her. Now there are four of us waiting for the AA.

It is completely dark and extremely cold. The wind pushes us around. Our noses are red from the cold, and we all have a halo of our own hair surrounding us, lit up each time a car zips past.

A few more police cars roar past.

A big bakkie slowly climbs the sidewalk behind Mackenzie's black Citroen. Two guys are here to rescue the damsels in distress.

"Naand dames." And of course they are Afrikaans.

They chat with us and ask what they can do. After explaining to them that we are waiting for the AA, due to the absence of a spare tire, due to my stupidity, they gallantly offer to wait with us. We insist it's not necessary, they insist that it is.

Our little group is growing. There are six of us.

"Mich! Why don't you just phone Jess and ask if you can use her spare tire?" Mackenzie suggests. Jess and I both drive Yarises.

"Do you think I can do that?" I ask skeptically.

"Well, it's going to save everyone a lot of time and money," she points out.

"That's true." I consider. It will be easier.

I phone Jessica.

"Jess, can Mackenzie please come and fetch your spare tire because otherwise I have to have my car towed and … everything. She'll be really quick and I promise to take my car in tomorrow morning so you'll have your tire back by tomorrow afternoon at the latest."

Pause.

"Ja, that's fine. But Mich, you really should have gotten your spare tire fixed."

"I know." I pause, bitter. I really did know that. I already felt like an idiot.

"It's just, it's really dangerous driving around without a spare tire, friend."

"I know," I say flatly.

"Okay, no it's fine. Ja, tell Mackenzie she can come fetch it."

Mackenzie leaves to fetch the tire, and I cancel the AA.

Manly Afrikaner man stays around as he assumes that we will need help when the tire arrives. His friend goes and sits in the bakkie, his hairstyle is getting messed up by the wind.

We huddle together for warmth and wait for Mackenzie. An ADT car halts behind us.

"Afternoon." An impressive man exits the vehicle. He is humongous, both in length and girth. We don't correct him to tell him that it's actually night.

"What seems to be the trouble?" He's wearing the khaki ADT uniform, and it stretches to bulging over his form. His police boots and military hard hat complete the outfit.

"I hit the curb, and now my tire's flat. My friend is bringing a spare and then we're going to change it," I say. Everyone else seems too intimidated to answer. He looks the situation and each of us over, and nods.

"I will help them sir, they are okay," Afrikaner man says.

ADT nods again.

He doesn't leave.

We wait for Mackenzie.

"I think we'll be okay now—my friend is bringing the tire," I tell ADT helpfully. I wasn't scared of him, and I wasn't offended by his presence, I just thought that maybe there was someone else who needed him more at that particular moment.

"I'll stay here until you leave safely," he points to the ground and leans against the car. That sentence touches me. I think it's the first positive moment I've had with any kind of law enforcement.

Mackenzie arrives victoriously, bringing with her the tire of hope and new beginnings, the most beautiful round object ever to behold.

ADT and Afrikaner man debate how to change the tire. Together, they go about getting the tools, removing the battered old tire, and replacing it with the new one. I have to explain to them how the damage to the front and rear of my car are from two separate incidents and not from the night in question.

We huddle, reduced to spectator status, even though we could have changed the tire. We watch the two men in the busy street. As they bend over my car, one jean-pant-clad bum and one impressively-uniformed-buff bum stick out into the darkness.

They are a team for no other reason than to help the girl on the side of the road.

"Flashbacks" is about as descriptive as a word can get. Judith, being fancy, calls it the "intrusion symptom." Some PTSD sufferers' flashbacks are so bad, they can't go about their daily life, they are so repeatedly interrupted with scenes from what happened. My friend emails me a while after we were raped and tells me about her nightmares—when she is drowning in the blood that came out of her vagina. I feel bad for her but relieved that my unconscious seems to be steering clear of the subject, until one insignificant week night. I sleep on the ground floor of our flat—the others all sleep upstairs. My room has its own sliding door that leads outside to a little garden. It also has Trellidors and blinds. The blinds are a bit broken and don't close all the way, so sometimes I fall asleep looking at the black slit. That night—a night no different from any other night—I dream about him.

I see his face and recognise it more clearly than I would my own. He's come to finish what he started. He's come to kill me. I know this because I was inside of him. I am part of the rapist. Just like he never left me, I never left him. But I am also me, lying in bed, unknowing, unsuspecting, sleeping. He creeps, silently, right to the slit where the blind gapes, the perfect frame for him to see my face. He never doubts where to go. Never hesitates. He doesn't have to recognise me. He has always known me. That's when he sees that both the glass sliding door and the security door are gone. He has his butcher's knife in his right hand. All he has to do is reach.

I breathe, smell, hear him, feel him. I startle awake and see him. The predatory whites in his eyes, his teeth, the glint of his knife, his nails as he reaches for what was left...

I gasp, really awake now. The sheets stick to me. I reach for my cellphone.

"Hello?" My mom answers instantly, almost as if she was waiting for my call.

"I dreamt ... he was here!" I sob, hysterically. "Mom, he was here and he ... came to ... kill me!"

I sob and chatter incoherently for a while, and my mom makes soothing noises. "You're safe. Do you hear me? He's not there. You're okay. You're safe," she repeats. After about ten minutes of repeating this mantra, she asks if I'm tired.

"Yes," I hiccup.

"Do you want to go sleep in Jessica or Ashley's room?" she asks.

"I ... I can't move," I tell her. It's the truth. I am frozen to the spot. The mere thought of trying to walk to their rooms and all the movement and danger that would entail and then to speak to them and explain what happened, exhausts me. And I don't feel like I can burden them with this. I hate putting stuff like this on them.

"Okay, okay. I'll stay on the phone with you until you fall asleep. Okay?"

"Okay. That sounds good," I say.

"Okay, good."

We put our phones against our ears, and I try to sleep. It's three-thirty in the morning. I can hear my mom breathing. Every couple of minutes she whispers, "You are safe. I am here. I love you."

I don't know how long it takes me to fall asleep—at least an hour. I don't once reply to her whispering. I know she kept on whispering long after I fell asleep.

I read that some women have the revenge fantasy where the role of the victim and the perpetrator are reversed. Those stories make good movies and books, like *The Girl with The Dragon Tattoo*. I really, really, wish I was one of them. Other women have the fantasy of forgiveness where the survivor imagines that she can transcend her rage and erase the impact of the trauma through a willed, defiant act of love. Those are usually the Christian women who wish to transcend their experiences, "but it is not possible to exorcise the trauma through either hatred or love," Judith says.

I feel like a lazy trauma survivor. I never have the desire for either revenge or forgiveness. I mostly forget that he exists. Even after I have the nightmare it was relatively easy for me to reduce him to nothing in my mind. What happened with André was

117

much more personal. I wanted to hurt him in cruel and unusual ways, for years. I wanted to tell his family and every girl he would ever date who he truly is and what he is capable of. I was in the process of writing him a very long and evil letter that I was going to send to him on Facebook when I was raped. Stranger raped.

I was against the death penalty before I was raped. I still believe that we don't have the power to decide whether someone else should live or die. I wonder, if my rapist ever came up to me and confessed, would I want to kill him? If he was remorseful, would I forgive him?

I imagine myself, sitting in a park, reading. He walks up to me. Same leather jacket. Same sneakers, with mismatched shoelaces.

"I raped you."

I look at him.

"I know." Because he is part of me.

What do I see? Remorse?

No.

I see arrogance.

I see pride.

He smiles. Then he turns around and walks away. Because he is free. He is free to live his life.

And I sit there. And I am rape.

I now know that I am capable of killing someone in the heat of the moment. I would do it to survive. But, as for what comes after it, whether any of me would be left over, I'm not sure about that anymore.

Malini started a blog around the same time that I did. One of her first posts was on the commencement speech that JK Rowling had given at Harvard. It rang very true for me. In it Rowling said that "failure meant a stripping away of the inessential. I stopped pretending to myself that I was anything other than what I was…"

That's how I feel about the rape. Not that it's a failure, but that it's removed all the parts of me that were unnecessary, all those parts that were there for show, all those parts that I used to put on display in order to make other people happy. I cut people out of my life who aren't good for me, something that is hard for me to do and that has to be done without bitterness. I stop caring what other people think of me, not just saying that I don't care but actually not caring. I stop needing to please other people. Rape uncovers my bare, essential self. She is deeper, darker, and a little bit twisted. And, for the first time in my life, I am fine with her. She is also clumsy, sarcastic, very, very weird, and loves to laugh. She cries when she reads something beautiful and gets more excited about Christmas than most children. She will also love you with all of her heart, dream impossible dreams, tease you with a smile, dance all night to one song on repeat, and lie next to you just to hear you breathe. She is rape. But she is not just rape.

JK Rowling also says, "Rock bottom became the solid foundation on which I built my life."

Rape, slowly, became the foundation on which I build my life.

Slippery motherfucker.

I slowly start to realise the other ways I've changed. I realise that people will always be able to hurt me with their words. One of the worst things that someone close to my family said after I was raped was:

"Maybe this will teach her to be more careful."

This, more than anything else, makes me feel that the rape was my fault. It was said behind my back, a cavalier statement never intended for the ears of the one it cut down. Lots of people are brave like that. It steals what fighting spirit I had built up at that point and tears me down, leaving me in a heap. I feel like I'm a stupid little girl who had "gotten herself raped" and now needs to be shunned by the community for her sins.

But no, I will never turn down a friend who needs to talk. I will never stop living my life. I will never lock myself in my house. I will never stop going out with my friends. I will never stop being me. I will never live a shadow of my life because some men out there choose to be rapists. And if you choose to blame me for living my life, that is your prerogative.

It's hard to forgive people for saying stuff like this. I do forgive them. But I never want them to be part of my life ever again.

In the midst of the monotony of day-to-day life, I try to be good to myself. I have one particularly memorable weekend. On Friday night I watch *The Bachelorette* with my housemates, a household tradition. We get into our pyjamas, make dinner, drink wine, and completely and irrationally dissect the contestants' lives.

"He looks poor, he shouldn't win."

"But he's got such a good heart!"

I stay at home on Saturday night when everyone else goes out. I make myself an ostrich steak with a pepper sauce and drink red wine while I watch a French DVD. When my friends ask me to go out, I don't suffer from my usual dread that I am missing out on life, or that I am punishing myself because of what I've been through and because I have no idea how to handle myself. Instead, I feel nurtured, like I am looking after myself. The silence starts to seep into my skin, the worms in my head lie down to sleep for a while. My emotions take a break from scraping against my flesh like sandpaper.

That Sunday morning it's grey, my favourite kind of day. I take my camera and my notebook with a pen and walk to the park. I love walking in winter. I feel like it brings out my true colours and agrees with me.

In the park, I am the only person who came alone with absolutely no purpose other than to be. Everyone else is there with a kid on the playground, walking their dogs through the trees, a partner, exercising, doing something. I amble around. Grey clouds tumble above, the brisk air cleaning me from the inside out. I have black hair, quite a big bag, and a ridiculous smile on my face. I am not offended when a yummy mommy takes her little boy's hand and walks a safe distance away from me.

I sit down on the bench in the park. That's when I see the squirrel, not even two metres away from me. Squirrels have always been significant in my life. When I was in Stellenbosch, I once asked God, if He loved me and was there for me, He would let me see a squirrel. Blind ignorance and youth. But I saw four squirrels that day and, for me, that was enough.

I didn't know, now, if it was God who sent this squirrel to me. I look at the little guy. His dark eyes inspect me. I am over-whelmed with wonder and happiness. He runs away. His tiny body makes this rad Mexican wave as he moves. I take out my notepad and write a poem. I haven't written a poem in a long time.

I am crying at the amazement of being able to feel something other than heartbreak. When I finally walk home, I thank whatever God there is for the wonder and magic that still exists in this world. And that I am still able to find pieces of it.

13.

MY BIRTHDAY IS ON THE 21ST of July, a Saturday. I'm dreading it. I usually love my birthday, and I celebrate it for about a week. But now I'm stuck on not knowing how I'm supposed to celebrate my life after nearly dying.

For my eighteenth birthday I threw a Moulin Rouge party. My mom hired two party planners and they cooked a three-course French meal. They also covered our sun room in a black tent and redecorated the table with a red tablecloth, white serviettes, and gold cutlery. I wore a maroon corset, and my mom was my pimp in a tux. Once my friends arrived, there was an abundance of fishnet-stocking-clad legs and cleavage. Mackenzie gave a speech that made me cry. There were also two very embarrassed topless teenage boys who were our waiters. I ate my caviar and drank my champagne while wearing long, black silk gloves.

That was a great night. But now my life feels so ... bland. I feel like my life is the life of a loser. I don't go anywhere or do anything. I just sit and feel sad and sorry for myself. I look on my computer screen and see friends travelling, getting married, basically just living.

A week before my birthday I'm doing grocery shopping when I have this thought, "I'm so fucking tired of feeling sorry for myself."

I put down the cheap cheddar cheese and walk towards the party section. When I get there a mom is helping a small boy choose candles. I clear my throat, and they move away so that I can grab a "Happy Birthday" banner.

At home on my bed, I cut the banner into four pieces, each

one shouting, "Happy Birthday!" I stick one on the mirror in the lounge, one on the fridge, another in the upstairs hallway and the final one in the bathroom so that you have to see it when you do your business.

That's better.

On Wednesday night, Jessica, Ashley, Mackenzie, and I go for sushi. It's a sunny evening so we go directly after work. We tell the manager it's my birthday, and I get a free dessert.

"But, you're still Michelle," Jessica insists when I try to explain to her how I've changed. People try very hard to hold onto the old me, but I'm not that person anymore, and I'm not even sure who this new person is.

"I'm not, Jess," I look into her innocent face, "I'm not that person at all. Rape defines every part of me, and I don't know how to explain it or why, but I can't even ride the lift at work without being scared that someone is going to rape me in the ten floors it takes to get upstairs. It's there, all the time."

Tears stream down her face. It's the first time she's cried about it in front of me. Sometimes I worry about how my rape affected her.

Jessica, Mackenzie, and I then go to &Union to drink beer and listen to the band. They make such an effort to make me feel loved. Mackenzie gives me a CD of music and even bakes brownies for me. Their love makes me solid. It makes me real.

As I walk to my car after work on the Friday, my breath starts to get shallow. My black leather boots crunch the dried leaves and small brown stones on the dirt road as I walk through the parking lot.

Dumdumdumdumdumdumdumdum.

My heart is inside of my head, slamming against it.

I can't breathe. I lean against a silver Honda and try to gulp the air, but instead yellow, green, and red spots fly in front of my eyes. As I heave and gulp, spit flies out of my mouth and falls onto the ground in long strands.

Great. A panic attack. After a couple of minutes, I slowly make my way to my car, open the door, and collapse into the seat.

I take out my phone.

"Hello?"

"Mom ... I can't ... breathe."

"Okay, I want you to put your head onto your arms and down onto the steering wheel. Then you need to count your breaths. You are okay."

Finally, she calms me down.

As I walk through the sliding door my phone beeps.

"Sorry I can't make it tonight friend. Have the best night and happy birthday!"

She's the third person to cancel. That leaves me, Ashley, Jessica, Mackenzie, and Julia. My body shakes as I walk to my room.

"Hey Michy!" Jessica says.

I shake my head and close the door. When I'm alone I just sit and stare at the wall. I had really needed people to show up tonight.

When Mackenzie gets home, she knocks on my door. "How are you?"

I shrug.

"Come sit in the lounge with us while we get ready."

Mackenzie makes me sit on the floor in front of her so that she can give me a massage. Her strong hands push and knead into my tired back. Jessica hands me a glass of red wine, which I slowly sip as it loosens the knot in my stomach.

We walk into Sidewalk Café where couples and small groups of friends are laughing over heaped plates and glasses of wine. The fireplace is lit, and there are succulents placed all over the restaurant. The wooden chairs and tables are close together, so we have to squeeze to get to our table. When we all sit down there are two empty chairs that we have to ask the waiter to take away.

I eat a pepper steak, and we talk about everyone's jobs. There are a lot of awkward pauses.

When we get to The Dubliner, my body is loose with alcohol. The live rock band plays too loudly for us to talk, so we dance in a circle on the packed dance floor. I walk to the bar by myself to get a shot.

As I knock back a tequila—no salt or lemon—a guy catches my eye. He's on the short side, stocky. A strong nose and dark, dark eyes. He's wearing skinny jeans and a plain black shirt.

"Hey," he smiles at me.

"Hey."

He takes my hand and leads me to the dance floor. His hand is hard, calloused. He pulls me close to him as we move together, his hands lightly touching my back. I stare at his eyebrows. There are some so long they curl at the ends. He smells like sweat.

He leans in.

"No," I say, and push him away.

He walks back to me and whispers in my ear, "Fuck off."

I walk away.

My mom, Janah, and I spend the whole day of Saturday doing wedding stuff for Janah and eating cake for my birthday. Janah is going to be the most beautiful bride in the world. She has a unique, vintage style. I am so proud of her because, despite the pressure of the wedding and her past where she was worryingly thin, almost anorexic, she is still enjoying food and not extreme dieting like other brides.

At the dinner table, Oom Theunis and my mom are coupled off on one side while George and Janah are coupled off on the other. I sit alone at the edge.

"On our first date, I prepared key cards with topics of conversation because I was so nervous," George tells us. He and Janah were acting like newlyweds, and four years into their relationship, it is extremely cute.

"Have you guys heard about the Higgs boson particle?" I ask the table, wanting to brag about the first-ever scientific knowledge I had read up on.

"Yes, it's a particle that gives you eternal life," Janah smirks. We all laugh and I proudly tell her the real meaning of the particle.

I look at George and Oom Theunis, and what strikes me the most about both of them are how they are beautiful, caring people and they love my sister and my mom respectively. Just to have a good heart can mean so much.

That night, Janah and George leave the hotel to go fetch her bag in their car. It is just me, my mom, and Oom Theunis sitting on the bed. I break down and cry while they hold me. I cry with my whole body, every inch of me burning with pain. I cry because I am alone and ashamed. I cry because I want to put what happened to me in a neat little box labelled "wisdom" from which I can draw pretty, folded envelopes to give to people.

But that's not going to happen. Not tonight.

It seems like every single day at work I am reading another story about rape that made the headlines. It starts with a video circulated on the internet of a mentally handicapped girl being gang-raped. Then I read about a girl in Australia where the man who was accused of raping her got off because she was wearing skinny jeans and the judge ruled that you can't rape someone who wears skinny jeans. Then I read a story in South Africa where the life sentence of a rapist got reduced to fifteen years because the victim accepted clothing and gifts from her uncle, the rapist. She also didn't scream.

I didn't scream.

A lack of resistance does not imply consent.

It is election year in the United States of America. Every Republican with a "grey face and a $2 haircut," as Tina Fey dubbed them, gives their opinion about rape.

Todd Akin states that if a woman is "legitimately raped" then her body has a way of preventing pregnancy.

Richard Mourdock states that rape is part of "God's purpose." Roger Rivard's father once told him "some girls rape easy," which was his response to the newspapers after being told that a girl was raped in a Wisconsin classroom.

Paul Ryan, who ran for Vice-President with Mitt Romney, refers to rape as "a method of conception."

Tom Smith states that getting raped and becoming pregnant is sort of like being the father of a daughter who has a baby out of wedlock.

I don't know how to respond to these things. I'm sad. Beyond everything else, I'm scared and hurt. I'm tired.

A stream gets started on Reddit where rapists could explain themselves by telling their side of the story. A lot of the stories could have been André's story. "I made a mistake..." or "I didn't think..." and every story is followed by hundreds of people saying, "You made a mistake—everyone makes mistakes, you're not a bad person!"

What really strikes me about this thread is that a lot of girls out there want a safe place to experiment sexually. They don't necessarily want to have sex, but they want to explore their sexuality and, in this way, their sexual agency. What goes wrong is when the young men perceive any slight sexual hint as an invitation for sex. The girl gets stripped of her sexual agency and becomes a mere passive respondent to the hormones and lust of the young male body. She learns at an early age that men only want sex. Nothing else is relevant.

Definitions of rape based on representations of sexuality where the male acts and the female reacts (says yes/no) are highly problematic. They are problematic because female sexuality is not merely reactive, just as male sexuality is not always driven by the need to initiate. On the thread on Reddit, more often than not, it is the girl who initiates the encounter. It is the guy who takes things too far.

Real statistics on sexual assault don't exist, because the girl thinks that she's to blame. She started it after all.

There is a practice in some parts of the world of stoning to death girls and women who have been raped for bringing shame onto their families. I think it is just as troubling that young women I know can't accept that being coerced into sexual intercourse by someone that they know despite the fact that they were drunk, dumb, flirting, or whatever, is still rape.

14.

THE ASSHOLE THAT FINALLY makes me say "enough" is named Dylan. Like all of my manly adventures this year, all it takes is one night.

Every Friday afternoon, we stop work at about four p.m. and drink a couple of beers. The last few weeks, I have been getting friendlier with a group of people from work, and one night we decide to go out after the beers run out.

I drink too much wine. Like always.

I hate myself again.

He seems so nice, so interested in me. I am such a fool. Again. I can't remember how I end up agreeing to go to his place. I can only remember being there. Naked, in bed. Then saying "No" again. He listens.

But when I try to get dressed and go home, he gets angry. He throws me out on the street. "I hope you find someone to deal with your fucked up shit" is his parting gift to me. He locks the door and walks away.

It is the middle of the night, I'm on a road that I don't know. I am still drunk. There are no taxis in sight. I'm alone. I try to buzz his apartment but I can't find him.

I phone everyone that I know—no one is answering. Finally, a taxi comes. I pretend to make a phone call to a friend to tell her that I'm on my way home, more for a false feeling of security than anything else.

The taxi driver looks at me strangely. Stares at me. I am a filthy whore. He is going to rape me as well. Why not? I clearly can't learn the lesson that I am meant to.

I talk to him. I make conversation and ask him about himself. I stop at the petrol station and buy him food and coffee. My body is poised for attack the whole time.

I make it home.

I keep putting myself in dangerous situations as if to test that I am still alive. I think I am unique in my stupidity but I learn later that this is something trauma survivors do. We re-create dangerous situations to prove we are still alive. When I can no longer stand one more second of my own company—when I am so weary of myself that I am ready to hurt myself—I drag myself to Jessica's room and climb into her bed. She sleeps with an eye mask on.

"Hey, it's me," I say as I slip into the sheets of someplace where I am worthy.

"Hey friend," she mumbles.

Seconds pass.

"Oh, my gosh, Mackenzie got mugged last night!" Jess sits up and yanks off her eye mask.

"What?" I turn around and face her.

"Oh my gosh, it was so bad. Ashley and I came home from The Power and The Glory and I was in bed when I heard a noise outside. It sounded like someone was laughing but when I leaned out of the window, it was Mackenzie. She was crying and convulsing."

"Shit, what happened?"

"She took a taxi home, the guy pulled over and drew a knife on her. So she said that she just threw her bag at him and got out of the car and ran home. It happened at the top of the hill so she sprinted about five hundred metres home."

"Fuck," I say.

"It was so bad when we got her, I only woke up because I heard her crying. But she was so hysterical I thought she was laughing. I have no idea how long she was outside before I woke up. Ash and I had to undress her and put her to bed."

We sit in silence. I stare at Jessica's white duvet. I am not shocked by the news. But I feel the inky spider steps of fear, hate, death running around my throat, my heart, my lungs. The knowledge of what near-death feels like. I am glad that I wasn't home to see her.

When I see Mackenzie she's like a shell. Shocked and numb. Angry and sad. A lot like me. I am so proud of her for running away, it's so much more than most people would have been able to do.

Later she admits that she didn't take a taxi. That she had been walking home when it happened. We all tell her how stupid that had been, but we don't have to. She knows. And I tell her about my night. Hadn't I been just as stupid? We sit there, the four of us. Thinking about how we get into these situations and how powerless we are to fight them. Society teaches us, "don't get raped" instead of pounding in the message of "don't rape." And here we are, four "don't get raped" girls and all we have is "being careful" to use as a weapon.

What would your life be like if you weren't scared? What would you do if you didn't have to 'be careful'? Even for women who haven't been raped, the fear of violence restricts their movements and freedom.

For our twenty-first birthdays Jessica and I travelled to Croatia. We spent the first week on a sailboat with twelve other people, sailing from island to island. We would dock at an island and then have the freedom to roam about.

Jessica and I would walk past the cafés that poured onto the cobbled streets, the hordes of people walking, the old buildings pressing up against each other, the clear ocean sparkling in the distance. The atmosphere was free and safe. We walked around all night long, and we never worried. We would speak to street vendors, cheerful waitresses, and anyone else. We stayed out until the sky was inky black and the streets held only a couple of people.

But we were never in danger. It was the most absurd feeling, to have the freedom to walk around, to move. To own the night.

I want to own the night again.

After Dylan kicks me out of his house with the hopeful message that I will "find someone to deal with my fucked-up shit," I've finally had enough. I don't know how or what I am going to do, but I know that I have to stop putting myself in situations where I lose control and allow men to treat me like dirt. I've been allowing men to treat me like a one night stand or not to come close to me at all. No more. I have been an idiot for way too long—it's time to take control.

I stop working in Cape Town and go back to Port Elizabeth. It's time to become me again.

On my last day at work, I look at the people there and wonder how they live their lives so full of missed connections.

I tell one guy, who has always stared at me, that I'm leaving. He says: "If only I had known it was tonight..." *You would have what?* I wonder.

How many missed connections make up a life?

I don't understand. Why do people always let life pass them by? Why do they never act on anything? I practically throw myself at another guy and tell him to come out with us. I find him interesting because he's serious and witty at the same time, and because he's religious. He's a Muslim, and I watched him fasting during Ramadan. I admire it. I like that he's devoted to his spiritual life. He never shows up.

There's a destructive force about being young, about figuring out what you want to be and what you want your life to be. I wonder how anyone makes it out alive.

That night I dance with my work friends in a bar. Until I look at them and feel disillusioned, like we are all trying too hard to be people we aren't. Like we are lying, not to each other, but to ourselves.

I wonder if anyone else notices it. In spite of this, I leave work with a sense of completion. The job gave me all that it could. Structure, routine, a reason to get up in the morning. I couldn't have handled pressure this year. When I walk out of the office for the last time at the end of August, I find that I don't want to look back.

I drive out of Cape Town on my favourite kind of morning: grey and misty with just the slightest whisper of a drizzle. I scratch my injured knee. Two weekends previously I had fallen, tripping over a leaf on the way out of the gate of our apartment. Mackenzie and I had been on our way out on the Saturday evening.

131

I was wearing black jeans and some of the material got stuck underneath a fold of skin as I landed my whole bodyweight on my knee. I let the tears of pain flow as I put on another pair of jeans to go out. We were going for burgers.

At Café Royale, I went to the bathroom to inspect the wound again. I lifted the piece of skin with a pair of tweezers and shuddered with pain. We had bought some Dettol on our way to the restaurant, and I put some on it. Underneath the top layer of skin congealed red blood cells stared at me. I bandaged my leg up again and went to eat my burger.

I had to go to the Mediclinic twice for the wound. When they asked what happened I said "nothing," because I was just being myself. It doesn't bother me anymore. I know it's going to leave a horrible scar but that's just part of me being me.

I put my car into gear and face the empty road, filled with the knowledge of who I am, unable to hide it anymore. No matter how battered or bruised I am—I am okay with being me.

The body seeks truth. I have experienced this in various ways this year. I become physically ill when I have to tell someone that I was raped. My body reacts negatively to people who have not dealt with what happened to me. I can only give a small part of myself to those who don't know what happened to me.

In order to survive, we all tell lies. Because of the enormous human capacity for self-deception, we may fail to recognise when we are lying, or when we are living authentically.

We all have the basic human right to keep quiet about something that is only our business. In the name of privacy, we don't have to share all of our experiences with each other, but privacy and secrecy are dangerous in a patriarchal society. They keep us trapped and perpetuate false myths about women. We think there's something wrong with us instead of turning the microscope on society. It's when we realise we share experiences that we can challenge old lies and create space for a new truth.

There is joy in making the private public, the shameful silly, and the personal political.

Someone said: "Some things are better left unsaid" with regards to my writing about my rape. In our culture, where people go out of their way to shock and to be perverse, does our apathy really mean that some things are better left unsaid or does it just mean that society is desensitised? Sometimes people use shock so that people will think about a phenomenon in a different way, but this is not my aim. Honesty is my aim, to honestly portray what rape is, for one girl, in the rape culture of South Africa. And if you don't think that deserves to be portrayed in a country where almost every woman can tell a story about how they or someone they know personally has been affected by rape, then, honestly, what is worth talking about? What is there that is worth fighting for?

I want to reclaim my status as someone who was raped. I am sad for those people who find it easier to judge my actions than to judge the actions of a rapist. I am not in the wrong.

15.

BACK IN PORT ELIZABETH, I find myself settling into the comfort of a solitary routine. I withdraw deep inside myself and, instead of seeking acceptance and love from men, I start to accept and love myself.

I decide to start horse riding again. I am nervous to start as I haven't ridden properly in seven years but I also know it is like riding a bike: once you learn it never really goes away. I take a lease at a rescue yard where the horses live outside in a herd. A lot of them are abandoned and troubled horses, some are old and some are unwanted. The yard is scrappy, with chickens and a sheep roaming about. The horses are underfed, with thick, clumpy coats, cracks in their hooves, and ticks all over their skin. I can ride whichever horse I want to until I find my favourite. I'm immediately attracted to a Palomino pony called Shannahan.

At the same time, I start reading a book called *The Tao of Equus*, by Linda Kohanov, which speaks about the healing power of horses and about a woman who uses her horses in her practice of psychotherapy. She speaks about the transformative power that horses have, something that she has experienced time and time again in her work.

I park my car and walk up the sandy hill that leads to the stables. The morning sun stings my eyes while the birds sing in the bushes surrounding me. When I reach the stables, the horses are lazing around in the shade hiding from the relentless beat of the sun. One of the ponies, Prince, a chestnut, is always a little removed from the rest. He comes up confidently to greet me.

Ears pricked, he touches my hand in a gesture of friendship and then starts to lick it—a peculiar habit.

I giggle. I go into the tack room and get Shannahan's halter. He is a friendly pony, and once he caught onto the fact that I always come with apples he readily walks to me, leaving his friends behind once he sees me. I am fully aware of the fact that this is bribery and not affection. In order to show the other horses that I am not a threat, I approach them at a 45 degree angle, avoiding their gaze. When they reach out their noses to touch me, they are acknowledging me and accepting me into their space.

As horses can only communicate in body language and feelings, it is very important to be aware of what you are feeling at all times as they will immediately pick it up. As herd animals, they will always want a leader. When it is just you and your horse, he will always be testing you in order to establish who is the leader. For example, if he turns his shoulder or hind-quarters to you, he shows that he does not respect you.

Horse riding again meant that I had to teach myself to be strong, assertive, and a leader. I couldn't give in or back down. I had to face physical challenges head-on. I tackle Shannahan up, aware that he is a champion show jumper. I marvel at his energy. His friendliness borders on bossiness, and he is not convinced that I am his leader. As we trot around the ring I start to smile.

Nervously, I cue him to canter. He takes off at full speed. I pull at the reins as hard as I can, aware that this won't make any difference. He is out of my control. The only thing that will calm him down is to ride him in circles, but I'm afraid that the arena is too small. I have no idea what to do.

I finally manage to stop him, but by now my heart is in my throat and he is teeming with nervous energy. I wasn't in charge. He felt my lack of control, my nervousness, and decided to run off. He didn't want me off: he could have bucked if he wanted that. He just wanted to go faster. He was testing me and teaching me at the same time.

Just like Shannahan, I had been running away the whole year. Running headlong into things that I knew nothing about and that could hurt me, acting in dangerous ways despite knowing better. Next, I try Delamont, a beautiful bay mare, tall and skittish. I have to be extra calm around her, which teaches me to become more aware of my emotions. One day my heart is beating rapidly because I am excited about a new route where we could gallop and she skitters away. I have to walk and calm myself down before she lets me stroke her. She teaches me to become aware of myself again, to gauge where I'm at before I go jumping into things, to not just feel my emotions but to acknowledge them and conquer them.

A lot of the time I go to the yard and just hang out with the horses, watch them, and be with them. A little pony, Liquorice, decides that he is going to follow me around and be my best friend. After following me from a safe distance the first day, he is always right behind me. He barely reaches my shoulder, but when I walk, he walks. When I stop, he stops. I scratch him and take off his ticks. He tickles me with his lips. He teaches me to enjoy every moment and to ask for what you want.

One day, as I am hanging around with the horses, two girls come and ask me if I want to join them for an outride. They take two of the little ponies, I saddle Deli. We go for a two-hour ride to the beach. I'm nervous as we make our way to the beach and speak a lot of nonsense to the other girls. Despite this, Deli calmly follows my commands.

When her hooves hit the sand, a smile stretches onto my face. I kick her into a gallop. We fly across the white sand, the waves exploding next to us. I inhale the salt air as it nudges us on and the power of the horse seeps into me. On her back, I am strong. I am in control. I am happy. We gallop away our worries with the sea breeze in our hair. And I feel like I am free.

During the day, I write and spend time with my mom and the dogs. I find myself laughing all the time: when Piccadilly tries to jump on my bed and misses or when Nemo eats Lindt chocolate out of the wrapper. I laugh when I am by myself, just because I can.

I go out with two friends and I don't drink. I find that I am even crazier sober than I am drunk. Who knew? I stop binging and punishing myself with food. I realise what it means to nurture myself.

My mom and I buy pepper spray and a Taser gun for me. Way late, I know, but better late than never. Just knowing that I have these on me gives me a renewed sense of power, a sense of not being such a helpless victim. Of knowing I can fight back.

I feel like I was reconnecting with what is real, with what is important and what is me. I still feel the constant presence of fear. Judith talks about how trauma victims are often keenly aware of their continued vulnerability to threats and reminders of the trauma. At the stables, I am mostly alone. One day, a man comes looking for his brother. He has a confident swagger that screams danger, and I am scared.

I go jogging for the first time since I was raped. My usual route is a couple of blocks around our house in Port Elizabeth. As I'm running, an alarm goes off at a nearby house. I keep running. Then another alarm goes off. And another. Despite my beating heart, I keep running. After a while the alarms stop. An ADT car screeches past me with its alarms on. I'm mad. How can I live my life if, every single time I try and do something that empowers me, it goes wrong? Instead of jogging the shortcut home, I keep running. I refuse to let someone scare me. Maybe I want to re-establish a degree of control over my own bodily and emotional responses, to reaffirm a sense of power. But after that day, I don't ever want to go jogging again.

I learned that not all danger is overwhelming, that not all fear is terror—that's Judith again. I find myself permanently in a state of readiness for attack, but it is not out of fear. It is rather out of a grim determination that no one else will ever take control of my body ever again. I am in control now, and that is the way it will stay. I know exactly what I will do if someone ever tries to attack me, and I feel sorry for that person.

In Judith's book, *Trauma and Recovery*, it states that, once the survivor no longer feels possessed by the traumatic past, she is in possession of herself. Her task becomes to become the person that she wants to be. In that process, she draws upon those aspects of herself that she most values from the time from before the trauma, from the experience of the trauma and also from the recovery. Integrating all of these elements, she creates a new self, both ideally and in actuality.

I realise, slowly, that as I am writing I am becoming not a "victim" or a "survivor" but just more of me.

I find myself as I walk along the green pastures with the sun shining and the horses surrounding me as friends do. The dirt on me is real earth, not the superficial sweat and grime from the city. I see the yellow, purple, and orange flowers blooming along our path. I am consciously redefining who I am and becoming more comfortable with that person.

Being back in PE gives me peace. The quietness of sleeping late, horse riding, writing, spending time with my mom, my stepdad and my dogs allows a steady certainty to form inside of me. When I reflect on who I am, I have an image of a rock at the beach. Waves wash over me. While before the rape, I was malleable, more eager to please, now I am stronger and more sure of who I am. As Judith Herman states, I can recognise the positive aspects that came out of being raped while also acknowledging that they came at too great a price. Sometimes I am scared of not being seen as "the victim" anymore. When you are the victim, people make special allowances for you. It's hard to move out of this space, to take the step towards self-actualisation that tells people that you are stronger now. That, even though you aren't okay every single day, you are more okay than not okay.

I miss my friend. I miss her company and her heart. I miss laughing with her. I message her and tell her that. She tells me she is doing well. I hope it is the truth.

I go back to Cape Town to throw my sister a flapper-themed bachelorette party with her friend Natalie. We hold it at her flat. As usual, I go overboard. I order about twenty-five vintage cupcakes, food platters, and at least one champagne bottle for each girl and a couple to spare. I wanted to hire fire jugglers and an ice bar, but Natalie convinced me that was going too far. Natalie and I decorate with dried roses, candle-light, a giant champagne bottle, and fairy lights. I printed pictures from the twenties that we put up everywhere. I also download authentic 1920s music which we play through an iPod dock. We make up party packs for all the girls who will come, sweeties and long cigarette holders with cigarettes. I also buy my sister an outfit especially for the occasion.

Six of us gather on Natalie's balcony, chatting, laughing, smoking, and drinking champagne. We are all dressed in our 1920s finest. We pose for photos and toast to Janah and George.

"So, what was his pick-up line?" Natalie asks.

Janah is blooming as a result of all the attention.

"He said, 'aren't you tired of men leaving you, because I never will.'"

Simple, direct, honest, cutting through all the bullshit layers of being young and confused. As the night goes on, we do burlesque dancing. We play the "how well does Janah know George" game and I show them the monkey that George told me he thinks Janah looks like.

When we go out, a man tries to flirt with Janah, "I'm getting married!" she shouts at him.

16.

JANAH AND I STAND OUTSIDE her wedding venue, waiting for the right time to enter. I look down into her green eyes, a lighter shade than mine. I think back to how she had to leave Port Elizabeth for her first year at Stellenbosch barely a week after Roneldi died. I remember how we used to be so close that it never occurred to us to knock before entering each other's rooms, how we would just sit together, doing nothing.

I remember how she once said to me when she was sixteen: "If things get too bad at home, I'll take you and we'll go away." She was going to take me to America so we could become famous. I remember how she used to drink wine at night in order to fall asleep because she was so alone. She used to talk about how she would have lots of lovers but never get married.

A lot of my friends doubt whether they are with "the one." I asked Janah how she knew George was the one when she got engaged. "I just do," she said, the most fuss-free answer I've ever heard.

The sun is streaking through the clouds but the day is cold. It had been raining the whole week. We are on a rustic wine farm in Stellenbosch, green vineyards surroundings us on all sides and craggy mountains in the distance. The building is simple, red brick on the outside; inside, it is a mixture of industrial and vintage ruin with wooden beams, cement floors, and holes in the walls.

Janah is breathtaking. Her dress, a work of art that she helped design, has an intricate lace gold corset, a chiffon overlay, puffed-up sleeves, and a tight-fitting soft skirt that flows over her body. She has red lips and nails.

My dad is standing with us, taking photos. He will walk Janah down the aisle. I still haven't met my sister, Emma, who is over a year old by now, but I know she is inside with my stepmother Ioanna.

The harmonisation of two little girls' voices ripple through the chapel at the top of the building. Their rendition of "Ave Maria" has most people in tears as my incandescent sister floats down the aisle, my dad's arm seemingly the only thing still holding her to this earth. The low lights and the mason jars with candles are burning with life.

Through laughter and tears, my sister and George promise their lives to each other. My body sings with happiness for my sister, who so bitterly spoke about marriage, who didn't believe in true love, who was hurt by men over and over again in her life, and I am in awe at the wonder of two real, broken people finding love that they want to make last for a lifetime.

Holding hands as we witness their love, they swing their palms back and forth like two children playing at getting married.

Everyone is crying.

When they are being congratulated, George comes over and hugs me. "Sussie!" he greets me. And he hugs me tighter.

"Boetie!" I reply.

Mackenzie is my date, and the wedding brings together just the right amount of strange people. At one stage, I am talking to Gavin, who was Roneldi's boyfriend when she passed away.

I meet Emma, my sister, a little one-year-old blonde girl. In her mother's arms, it is strange to think that she is my blood. She doesn't look anything like Janah or Roneldi or I did. Her features are softer, more open.

Or maybe that's just because she's a baby, you idiot, I think.

My dad swears that she looks just like me while my mom questions that we are sisters at all. I try to play with her but I find it hard to find this baby interesting when I have no idea who she is. I don't have the love for her that I have for the rest of my family. I desperately hope that changes. As Emma squeezes my thumb, I notice Ioanna, her mom and my dad's new wife, looking at me.

"You know, I can fix your scar for you," Ioanna says.

I have a scar on my cheek from when a dog bit me when I was five years old. The scar is so much part of my face that I don't even see it anymore.

"Really?" I ask, horrified.

"Oh, yeah. I can just inject a filler. I should have brought them over from Canada," she scrutinizes me. "The one on your forehead as well."

That scar is from when I fell on a chair.

"It's okay," I say.

"No, it's so quick and easy. I do a lot of cosmetic work now. Look, my lips are twice the size of what they were." She pouts in demonstration.

"I hadn't noticed," I lie.

I slowly back away. The rest of the night I imagine her staring predatorily at my scars every time I pass her.

The food is decadent, and the speeches are genuine and from the heart. An overwhelming feeling of love permeates the occasion. The candle light and chandelier on the one long white dining table invoke the feeling of an era past.

Gladys, our domestic worker, and her friend Julia sing a song for Roneldi at the reception. They are dressed in traditional Xhosa attire, Gladys in orange and Julia in red. They have white dots painted on their faces. They close their eyes. Gladys' voice rings across the venue, echoes and reaches up to heaven where I see my sister looking down and smiling at us. Julia joins her and they harmonise in haunting words our family does not understand: just as we do not understand death or what happened to our sister or where she is. The only thing that is clear is the emotion, universal and transcending, speaking of love and loss, life and death and its inevitability.

When my mom walks up to the microphone to a song from *Fiddler on the Roof*, no one understands why. She is so overcome with emotion that she gives what George later describes as a "mafia-style" speech. This consists of saying people's names and staring at them menacingly with such overwhelming emotion that the recipient has no choice but to break down and cry.

When Janah says her speech, she dedicates a song to my mom: *We All Stand Together* which my mom used to make us all perform when we were small. When my mom hears this, she abruptly starts dancing with her friend, Tannie Christa, and then starts crying so much that her mascara is on her chin and her forehead. While I run over to clean her face, she asks my stepdad, "Is my make-up okay?"

He looks at her.

"No," he says truthfully.

She wipes her fingers underneath her eyes.

"Better?"

"Yes," he lies.

When I make my toast to Janah, everyone laughs. I say that I have never known anyone who makes mistakes with such audacity, and that she has the amazing ability to follow her dreams, make mistakes, and always take the road less travelled. I also tell about how she once, while we were watching a movie, made a comment about how Johnny Depp was as timeless as a pearl. Unfortunately, he wasn't in the movie.

After we eat, we move to the dance floor. I feel welcomed and loved by everyone. At one stage I'm dancing with my mom, my step-grandmother with her walking stick, George's grandmother with her walker, Gladys, and Julia. Karen, one of my sister's friends, slaps my mom's bum. I think my mom is the biggest hit on the dance floor, perfecting what we all referred to as her mini-butterfly move, complete with forward motion Egyptian head bump. Natalie dances with one of George's friends so violently that we are exposed to her lusciously pink underwear. Thereafter she disappears and we don't see her again until the next day.

Mackenzie and I hang out with the smokers at the fireplace. Karl, the MC, flirts elaborately with her and then asks George for her number. Karl is a lecturer in English at UCT and has curly black hair and frequently speaks about "the revolution."

At one stage, Gladys comes with a cigarette. She puts her hand on her lips to indicate my silence. I nod and smile at her. Then, without warning, she shoves her head, with her elaborate traditional headpiece, into the fireplace to light her cigarette.

"Gladys, no!" Mackenzie shouts.

Before she catches fire, Mackenzie offers her a lighter.

At that moment, I see that Karen is on the dance floor but that she is looking peculiar. I can see her red underwear underneath her fishnet stockings.

Because she is no longer wearing a skirt.

Shit.

I run to her. I see her skirt lying on the floor next to her, and I grab it.

"Karen," I say as I would to a little girl.

She is shaking her body and moving in circles. I run after her, holding the skirt in front of me.

"Karen, can you put on your skirt?" I ask her.

"No, it's okay, everything's okay." She pats my back as if she was aware of some bigger secret about life and felt sorry for me about my ignorant, skirt-wearing ways.

I tried another tactic.

"Look at this pretty skirt!" I say, holding it up, "I think you'll look hot in it!"

"Okay," she shrugs and puts in on.

I turn around. On the other side of the dance floor, Karl the MC and my cousin Julie are, and there is no other phrase for it, viciously making out, pawing and groping each other as though their lives depended on it. I see a tongue more than once. I am confused, as he was just flirting with Mackenzie and buying us shots. I hear animal growl sounds in my head.

Janah and George are the last to leave, wrapped up in each other, celebrating their love. And I think, wow, what an awesome love story.

A year to the day, I wake up with tears clinging the corners of my closed eyes. I open my eyes and they fall. I stare into Piccadilly's loving gaze, and she knows. She loves me. Healing is not a linear path, and I am still sad.

It is midday and the sun is shining but the wind is howling like it's mad at the sun for coming out today. It is not a warm day but the sun refuses to go away. I decide to take a bath. There is something honest about a bath, how you are confronted with your body in a way you never are when you shower.

You are forced to be still, quiet with your body, yourself. I tap the water scalding hot. I throw in a few bubbles, not too much, I want to be able to see myself. I throw in some bath lotion. I climb in, and my body burns and burns and burns. I turn red all over. The water is green, and a few white bubbles emerge at the edge of the tub. I take a rough yellow sponge and wash myself. I wash my feet. My toes are painted red, not a bright red but almost black because that's the colour I prefer. I scrub my calves and knees, which are covered in scars, the most recent one still purple. I wash my thighs, slightly thinner than they were a month ago. I wash the stretch marks on my hips, the curve of my body. I rub myself with methodical, loving strokes, not brushing to clean but to appreciate, and observe, love and care. I scrub my stomach, scarred from operations, ignored and hated in the past. Mine. Not going anywhere. I love it and appreciate it. I wash my labia, the rough edges of the sponge scraping where I have touched myself and where I have been touched, where I have been hurt and betrayed, where I will be loved and caressed and pleasured. I wash the curve of my breasts. I wash every single spot on my body, and I love myself because I am worthy of my own love.

When I climb out of the bath, I am soft. So much softer than I was when I climbed in.

17.

A MONTH LATER I WALK to a green field in the Drakensberg mountains. It's on a farm and how I always pictured my healing place would look: grey clouds with bursts of sunshine, grass so green it makes every other green look faded. Soft sloping mountains, waterfalls, and misty clouds appear as if by magic. And at my feet, always a dog or a cat.

Let go of the fear. The voice is speaking to me again, the one who told me that I was going to get raped.

"If the horses come to you and want to interact with you, let them," Heather strides next to me, so at one with nature, you would never have seen her if it wasn't for her red hair and vibrant eyes.

"Okay," I say.

"It took a lot of guts for you to come here," she tells me.

"It took a lot of medication," I respond.

I'm sure I'm going to fail this. I know it's not a test.

I'm so going to fail this.

Earlier that day, we chose two horses to work with me, Pixie and Izzy. At Healing with Horses, the horses chose whether they want to work with you, everything here happens through mutual agreement.

We walk the rest of the way in silence. In the paddock, Izzy and Pixie, a black and a bay mare, stand next to each other, like they're waiting for me.

Which is a ridiculous thought.

As soon as I think this, they start walking in my direction.

Heather opens the gate, and I enter.

"Okay, okay, I'm going, I'm going!" she says, laughing.

She's talking to the horses, not me.

I turn to Izzy and Pixie, clutching to my chest the piece of paper where I wrote my thoughts.

I walk over a bit and sit on the edge of an overturned tractor tire. *Let go of the fear.*

Izzy comes and puts her black head over mine so completely that I can't see at all. She is protecting me.

In front of us, Pixie lowers her brown head to my side, until she's looking me in the eye.

For the first time in over a year, I let go of the fear.

I have never felt this safe.

How did they know?

The other horses in the paddock try to approach us, but as soon as they come close, Izzy chases them off, ears pinned back, tail swishing.

Then she chooses to walk back to me and again places her big, beautiful black head over mine. I am so enveloped by her presence I feel as if I never have to worry about anything ever again.

Pixie watches me as I cry with the shock and relief of being okay. Of being chosen. Of being loved. And a tear runs down her cheek as well.

They stand watching over me for twenty minutes.

They choose me, protect me, and stay with me. Because I needed them to.

It's then that I realise I am strong.

It's then that I realise I am brave.

It's then that I realise I am pure.

I want to leave you with this thought: it is wrong to turn your gaze to the women, the victims of sexual violence, who are wounded. I tell my story because no one else will. I tell my story because rape happens to everyone and no one talks about it. But I am not the one you should be studying.

Consider André, the man who thought I was joking when I asked him not to have sex with me because I was a virgin, who I had to comfort when he thought my broken hymen was proof of my positive HIV status.

Consider the man who threatened my life. Who made me put his penis into my body or "I will kill you." Who apologised for raping me before tying my hands and feet with shoelaces and leaving me on the rocks to die.

I was not bludgeoned. I was not stabbed. I was not gang raped. I was not subject to conditions of poverty and economic and social hardship while being physically abused.

But I was raped. I was raped, twice. Once by someone I thought was my friend and another time by a stranger. The fact that I am not the only woman to have been raped is what makes my story worth telling. If I was the only woman who was raped I would be extraordinary. But I am not. I am ordinary; I am one of many women who have been raped. My story is ordinary because too many women share my story. My story is worth telling because too many women identify with it. Too many women have first hand experience of what I am talking about. Yet it is the women who live with the shame. It is the women who are ostracised and blamed.

Consider them.

I am the statistic that I read about. I am the thing I always feared most.

I am rape.

There is no moral to this story, no life lesson, no motto or catch-phrase. There is simply a girl who lived through her worst nightmare and decided to try and hold onto her sanity by writing about it.

And I found love. In a hopeless place. *Kidding!* I found love in myself, in my family, in my friends. I found love in strangers, in beggars, in taxi drivers, and smiles, whispers, kind words, kisses, horse breaths, and doggy licks.

I hit rock bottom, and I was not alone.

So, I get to go on with my life.

My prize for surviving rape is that I continue to struggle. I get to wake up every day to live in an entirely unsatisfying world ... and to revel in those moments that take my breath away.

BIBLIOGRAPHY

Anderson, I. and A. Lyons. "The Effects of Victims' Social Support on Attributions of Blame in Female and Male Rapes." *British Journal of Social Psychology* 35 (2005): 1400–1417.

Anderson, I. "What Is a Typical Rape? Effects of Victim and Participant Gender in Female and Male Rape Perception." *British Journal of Social Psychology* 46 (2007): 225–245.

Anderson, I. and K. Doherty. *Accounting for Fape*. London: Routledge, 2008.

Burt, M. R. "Cultural Myths and Support for Rape." *Journal of Personality and Social Psychology* 38 (1980): 217–230.

Bohner, G., C. I. Jarvis, F. Eyssel and F. Siebler. "The Causal Impact of Rape Myth Acceptance on Men's Rape Proclivity: Comparing Sexually Coercive and Non-coercive Men." *European Journal of Social Psychology* 35 (2005): 819–828.

Bourke, J. *Rape: A History from 1860 to the Present Day*. London: Virago, 2007.

Gavey, N. *Just Sex? The Cultural Scaffolding of Rape*. London: Routledge, 2005.

Herman, J. (1992). *Trauma and Recovery: The Aftermath of Violence – From Domestic Abuse to Political Terror*. New York: Basic Books, 1992.

Kahn, A. S., J. Jackson, C. Kully, K. Badge and J. Halvoersen. "Calling it Rape: Differences in Experiences of Women Who Do or Do Not Label their Sexual Experiences." *Psychology Women Quarterly* 27: (2003): 233–242.

Lea, S. J. "A Discursive Investigation into Victim Responsibility in Rape" *Feminism & Psychology* 17 (2007): 495–514.

Lerner, M. J. "What Does the Belief in a Just World Protect Us From?" *Psychology Inquiry* 8 (1997): 29–32.

Lyon, M. "No Means No? Withdrawal of Consent During Intercourse and the Continuing Evolution of the Definition of Rape." *The Journal of Criminal Law & Criminology* 95 (2004): 277–314.

Levett, A. *Psychology Trauma*. Unpublished PhD thesis, University of Cape Town, Cape Town, 1989.

Moffett, H. "'These Women, They Force Us to Rape Them': Rape as a Narrative of Social Control in Post-apartheid South Africa." *Journal of Southern African Studies* 32 (2006):144–192.

Peterson, Z. D. and C. L. Muehlenhard. "Was it Rape? The Function of Women's Rape Myth Acceptance and Definitions of Sex in Labelling their Own Experiences. *Sex Roles* 51 (2004): 129–144.

Scully, D. *Understanding Sexual Violence: A Study of Convicted Rapists*. New York: Routledge, 1990.

Vogelman, L. *The Sexual Face of Violence: Rapists on Rape*. Johannesburg: Raven Press, 1990.

Wood, K., H. Lambert, and R. Jewkes. "'Showing Roughness in a Beautiful Way': Talk About Love, Coercion and Rape in South African Youth Sexual Culture." *Medical Anthropology Quarterly* 21 (2007): 277–300.

ACKNOWLEDGEMENTS

It's been five years since I started writing this book, and so many people helped make it happen.

Mom: thank you for teaching me to never take the easy way out. And thank you for never holding me back or making me feel like I have to censor myself. "But would your mom be okay with you writing this?" is not a question I ever had to ask myself.

Janah: your unconditional love and support has carried me throughout my whole life. I am so happy that you're my sister. To my dad, I appreciate dearly what you have done for me, I wouldn't have ever wanted anyone else to be my father. To my stepdad and stepmom, thank you for taking care of my parents after what happened to me.

My Lloyd: you taught me to trust and love again. There isn't really much to say except that you are a blessing and one of the most beautiful souls I have ever met. Thank you for always making me feel like it's okay to be me.

Ilze, Magdaleen, Candice, Monique, Natalie, and Lauren: thank you for so freely allowing me to share your part in my story. You're all my sisters. And badasses. Malini, you're my nihilist soulmate and my life would be less without you.

Carla: life coach, mentor, and killer of darlings. You are the

151

reason my babies are lying in a ditch and my book is so much better because of it.

Thank you to Susan Hawthorne for giving us permission to include her powerful poem, "How do you protect yourself from rape?" at the beginning of the book. Your poem resonates so strongly with me and, I'm sure, with many others.

To my work family Devaksha, Sarah, and Ziyaad: thank you for your unconditional support and for keeping me woke.

Thank you to my editor, Emily, who went on the journey of making this book worth reading with me. And Colleen, thank you for taking a chance on my story.

Thank you also to Inanna Publications & Education Inc. for taking a chance on this book. I never dreamed it would make it out of South Africa. Your choice to publish it validates the trauma of people who have been sexually abused throughout the world.

Michelle Hattingh was born in South Africa in 1988. She attended school in Port Elizabeth and studied Politics, Philosophy and Economics at Stellenbosch University. She went on to do her Honours in Psychology at Cape Town University and now lives in Cape Town. Her work has been published in *Elle SA, Marie Claire SA* and the *Mail & Guardian. I'm the Girl Who Was Raped* is her first book.